THE FINAL

MW00877800

CALL

Revelation Unmasked

A verse by verse journey through the

BOOK OF REVELATION

By

Dr. Don Boone

Printed in the United States of America

Copyright © 2017 by Dr. Don M. Boone

All rights reserved

ISBN-13: 978-1545589618

ISBN-10: 1545589615

All rights reserved. No part of this publication may be reproduced, stored in a retrieval system in any form by any means, electronic, mechanical, photocopy, recording or otherwise without permission of the publisher as provided by USA Copyright law.

First Edition

AUTHOR'S NOTE

While it has taken me years of study to complete this project, knowing that the Word of God never changes, historical events at this present time are changing. Many events are a fulfillment of the scripture passages found in the Book of the Revelation.

Events are tumbling over one another in such rapid succession that we cannot keep up with the pace in our everyday living. I do not want to date this book by the mention of names; however, I do want all the readers of this book to know that what may have been symbolic in the past could be literal right now. The world is full of FEAR and Terror seems to reign.

For the Christian we should rejoice in the knowledge that Jesus is Coming Soon! For the unbeliever, he or she must repent of sin and turn their lives over to the person of Christ-knowing that we are saved through Faith not of works lest any man should boast.

For our Nation, the beloved USA- we should get our houses in order- and our hearts. The lives of my children and grandchildren will never be similar to my childhood. We have gone so far so fast- the only answer to all our problems is

JESUS CHRIST. Get ready- do not be left behind to live under the rule of the antichrist and false prophet during the Tribulation Period.

Even so come quickly Lord Jesus!

REFERENCES

1. Expository Sermons on Revelation by Dr. W. A. Criswell

2. The Book of the Revelation by William R. Newell

3. Exploring Revelation by Dr. John Phillips

4. Riches of Revelation by Dr Ed Vallowe

5. Lectures on the Book of Revelation by Dr. H.A. Ironside

6. Guide to Survival by Salem Kirban

7. The Second Coming by Dr. M.R. DeHaan

8. Exposition Commentary by Dr. Warren Wiersbe

9. Daniel by Dr. Lehman Strauss

10. Pickings by Dr. R.G.Lee

11. The Second Coming of Christ by Dr. R.G. Lee

12. Agents of Babylon by Dr. David Jeremiah

13. Major Bible Prophecies by John F. Walvoord

14. Revelation Unveiled by W. Jim Britt

15. The Seven Last Years by Carol Balizet

ACKNOWLEDGMENT

This Book is Printed in Honor of the Legacy and Life of Rev. Rizcallah Constantine April 1, 1926- April 6, 2015

Special Thanks to:

Gabi and Kim Constantine

PCMAC, Inc.

Wayne Hudson

Brenda Tootle

Table of Contents

INTRODUCTION

The Book of the Revelation is a rich book. It is so sad today that many Christians look at this book as a sealed book. The Bible states that the Book of the Revelation is a book that should be unveiled. God never intended for this to be a sealed book. The book of Daniel was to be sealed to the end of time according to Daniel 12:9. The Book of the Revelation 22:10 states that we should not seal the sayings of the prophesy of this book for the time is at hand.

I know that this book was given for our instruction and our edification, it is sad that thousands of Christians are being robbed by a tremendous blessing in the area of prophesy because they are ignoring this book.

One of the reasons that most Christians ignore this book is because it is so pronounced, and symbolic, and many of them find it hard to understand. The purpose of this book is to make simple explanations concerning the Book of the Revelation in terms that laymen can fully understand. The book of Revelation is rich, it needs no vindication from me or any other author. I am not an authority on this book. The notes in this manuscript are written out of thirty years of preaching and teaching on the Book of the Revelation.

The word Revelation, Apocalypse means literally an unveiling or a manifestation. This book is the unveiling of our Lord Jesus Christ. It is His revelation to us. It represents him as the Son of Man in the midst of the churches during the present dispensation, and it represents Him as the Judge and the King in the dispensations to come. You will learn to appreciate Christ more when you read this book prayerfully, because it reveals Jesus as the Lamb who was rejected and will soon reign in Glory on the Throne!

The Book of the Revelation if you will observe when looking at the title is not in the plural form. People often speak of the Book of Revelations. There is no such book in the Bible. It is the Revelation, and it is one blessed continuous manifestation of God's unique Son as a Priest, a Prophet and a King. The book of the Revelation is the crowning book of the Bible. Since I know that the Word of God is absolutely perfectly unbroken; and unbreakable in the circle of all dispensational time; there are many comparisons that can be seen in the book of the Revelation.

A comparison in Genesis and Revelation will show how we have the types in Genesis and the completion of the truth in the book of the Revelation. So in Genesis we have the beginning and in Revelation we have the consummation.

(Creation)

* In Genesis 1:1; In the beginning that God created the Heavens and the earth.

* In Revelation 21:1; I saw a New Heaven and a New Earth.

* In Genesis 1:10; He gathered together the waters and called them the sea.

* In Revelation 21:1; The sea is no more.

* In Genesis 1:5; darkness he called night.

* In Revelation 21:25; there will be no night in heaven.

* In Genesis 1:16; God made two great lights the sun and the moon.

* In Revelation 21:23; the Heavenly City has no need of sun or the moon.

(Death)

* In Genesis 2:27; In the day that you eat thereof you shall surely die.

* In Revelation 21:4; That death shall be no more.

* In Genesis 3:16; I will greatly multiply your pain.

* In Revelation 21:4; Neither shall there be pain any more.

* In Genesis 3:17; Cursed is the ground for your sake.

* In Revelation 22:3; There shall be no more curse.

* In Genesis 3: 1 & 4; Satan appears as a deceiver of mankind.

* In Revelation 20:10; Satan disappears forever.

* Genesis 3:22-24; Adam and Eve were driven from the Tree of Life.

* In Revelation 22:2; The Tree of Life is assessable again.

* In Genesis 3:24; Adam and Eve were driven from God's presence.

* In Revelation 22:4; They shall see His face.

(Home)

* In Genesis 2:10; Man's early home was by a river that God created.

* In Revelation 22:1; man's eternal home will be beside the river in Heaven that God created.

Genesis gives us the creation of the Heavens and the Earth and of course Revelation presents a New Heaven and a New Earth. Genesis shows us the earthly paradise with the Tree of Life and River of Blessing lost because of sin and through the power of sin.

Revelation gives us the Paradise of God with the Tree of Life and the pure River of Water of Life proceeding out of the Throne of God and the Lamb. Paradise is regained for us in the Book of the Revelation through Jesus Christ's Atonement.

In Genesis we see the first man and his wife set over all God's creation, in Revelation we behold the second man and his bride ruling over a redeeming world.

In Genesis we are told of the first sacrificial lamb, in Revelation once slain Lamb is in the midst of the throne.

In Genesis we learn about the beginning of sin when the serpent first entered the garden of light to beguile Adam and Eve. In Revelation that old serpent called the Devil is cast into the lake of fire which burns forever and ever on out into eternity.

In Genesis we have the first murder, the first polygamist, the first rebel, the first drunkard. In Revelation all such who refused to accept God's grace in Jesus Christ are banished from His presence forever.

In Genesis we see man's city, in Revelation we see the city of God.

Genesis shows us how sorrow, death, pain, and tears of Sin and rebellion come into this world. The Book of Revelation does not close till we have seen God wiping away all tears and welcoming His redeemed into a home where there will be no more sin, no more death, no more pain, and no more sorrow forever.

It is not my intention in this book to deal with the field theological realm of thinking as to list the preterists or the futurists. It is my intention to open up the understanding of the meaning of this book as printed in the Word of God. There are varied schools of interpretation founded on the apothosists of how we read this and how we read symbols of this book. It is not my intention to present this as a theological dissertation. I am well aware that I am not an authority on this book therefore I know that this book is very symbolic. It is my understanding and intervention through this book to help you see God's mind after you read a portion of His Work and study with prayerful attention to every part of this book, and God will reveal the truth in His Word.

I am a futurist, that is, I believe the beginning at the fourth chapter of the Book is an apocalypse of the consummation of the ages described.

OUTLINE
"Systems of Interpretation"

Prophecy related to God

It is not out of order to set forth some basic reasons for students of the Bible to be interested in the study of prophetic themes as found in the Book of the Revelation. Christians Bible Students should be interested in prophecy because of who God is. In these last days, God is absolutely Sovereign… and He is carrying out His plan to perfection, despite man's involvement and gift of "FREE WILL".

A Study in prophecy related to God, proves that part of God's plan are being, and have been fulfilled in demonstration of the fact that God is TRUTH, and HE IS SOVERIGN! I often remind the people of God of this fact: "He is not worried concerning the future!"

Prophecy related to Scripture

Prophecy that is already fulfilled serves as a strong proof of the accuracy and truth of the scripture. Since God's servants are appointed to declare the whole counsel of God as listed in Acts 20:27; then we must be students of prophecy knowing that sixteen books in the Old Testament and one-twentieth of the New Testament Books are prophetic. Preachers who never preach on prophecy are robbing their people of the "Whole Word" of God. All of God's word must be ours, it cannot be slighted!

Prophecy related to Believers.

The study of prophecy will "fire up" a church! It will cause the believers not to follow false doctrines and false hopes, preached and taught by fallen prophets. It will cause the believers to look more at the groom (Jesus), instead of looking at the bride (church). This will bring the reality of Heaven into view, and bring peace of heart and mind, knowing that God's plan is on His time sheet, and it is perfect. The Believer's future is secure and certain, and he can lift up his eyes, for his redemption draweth nigh!

Premillennial Systems

As true in many points of theology, not all premillennialists agree in every point of their system. The word (Millennium) comes from the Latin word (Mille) (Thousand), and (Annus) (year). This word is not found in the Bible although its Greek equivalent appears in Rev. 20:2 – "A Thousand Years".

Premillennialists believe and hold to a literal interpretation of the scripture. At the close of this age, they believe that Christ will return for His church, meeting her in the air, (called the Rapture or Translation). then this will usher in the Tribulation Period which will last seven years. At the conclusion of the seven years, Jesus will return to establish His Kingdom on the earth for a thousand years, during which time the promises to Israel will be fulfilled. I am a premillennialist without apology.

Postmillennialism System

This system was taught by Daniel Whitby (1638-1726). It teaches that the second coming of Christ will FOLLOW the thousand year reign. However, the progress of evil has been so great in the past few decades that this theory has been brought in to disrepute. The social gospel was born from this system.

Amillennialism System

This system teaches that the only visible coming of Christ will be for judgment. There will not be two resurrections with an intercalary time of a thousand years between them. This system was born out of the Roman Catholic Church. This system teaches that the church is the Kingdom, and therefore is reigning now. If you would like to know more on this subject, study the teaching of Augustine. Amillenniaists today believe that a "Thousand" is the number of perfection or completion, and it is a symbolic reference to the complete period between the two advents of Christ.

DEFINITIONS

Abomination of Desolation - Desecration of the temple by the Antichrist. This will be his final attempt to force the Jews to worship him.

Matthew 24:15

"Therefore when you see the 'abomination,' spoken of by Daniel the prophet, standing in the holy place" (whoever reads, let him understand),

2 Thessalonians 2:3-4

Let no one deceive you by any means; for <that Day will not come> unless the falling away comes first, and the man of sin is revealed, the son of perdition, {4} who opposes and exalts himself above all that is called God or that is worshiped, so that he sits as God in temple of God, showing himself that he is God.

Daniel 9:27

Then he shall confirm a covenant with many for one week; But in the middle of the week He shall bring an end to sacrifice and offering. And on the wing of abominations shall be one who makes desolate, Even until the consummation, which is determined, Is poured out on the desolate."

Antichrist - The Antichrist is a name taken from 1 & 2 John. In Daniel, he is referred to as the little form and the "vile person". In 2 Thessalonians he is referred to as the "son of Perdition". In the Book of Revelation he is referred to as the "Beast out of the Sea". Satan so completely possesses this man that He is the incarnation of Satan in the flesh. The Antichrist will oppose Christ and the Saints and the Jews and he will first be hailed as a man of peace and given unlimited power. The Antichrist will only be a man at the very beginning of his reign but he will have Satanic powers. His sudden sensational rise as the Savior of the world threatened by destruction will be one of the marks of the beginning of the end of time. He will later attempt to annihilate all Jews and of course bring about his own defeat at Jerusalem by the return of Jesus Christ. The antichrist is a political figure in the book of the Revelation.

The False Prophet- The False Prophet will be a religious ruler who will undergird the work of the Antichrist. Both of these men will get their power from Satan. In the Book of the Revelation this is the picture of the Satanic Trinity.

1. The Antichrist

2. The False Prophet
3. Satan

The False Prophet will never attempt to promote himself, he will never become an object of worship. He will do this work of the prophet in that he directs attention away from himself to the one who he says has the right to be worshipped, which will be the Antichrist. The False Prophet will imitate many miracles of God. He will cause fire to come down from heaven, copying the miracles of Elijah in order to convince the nation Israel that he, is the Elijah that Malachi promised that is yet to come.

When he achieves this deception, he will declare that since this miracle, (bringing fire down from heaven), shows that he is Elijah; therefore, the Antichrist is truly the Christ that should be worshipped. He will build a statue and through some satanic miracle, he will cause the statue to talk and somehow come to life. When the people see this miracle they will fall down and worship the Antichrist, believing him to be Christ. I believe that at this point, Satan will totally become the Antichrist in the flesh.

Mark of the Beast- During the second half of the seven years tribulation period the Antichrist who was setting himself up as the "Man of Peace" will suddenly move against the Jews and all those who have accepted Christ during the first three and a half years of the tribulation period. In Revelation 13: 16-17 we read that the False Prophet will cause both small and great, rich and poor, free and bond to receive some mark in their right hand in on their forehand.

No man will be able to buy or sell unless he has this mark. Therefore those who refuse to submit to the authority of this system by having this mark either starve to death slowly or else they will be killed by representatives of the one world government.

It is possible that this mark could be a computer chip that is available on the market today with a complete history of the person's finances, medical and personal background. The chip can be implanted by a needle underneath the skin surface.

Rapture- The word Rapture refers to the time prior to the start of the seven year tribulation period. If you would like to learn more about the word Rapture, please read the section in this book that deals with Premillennialism, Postmillennilism, and Amillennialism. The word Rapture is not used in the Bible. It is taken from the Greek word meaning – "caught up".

The Book of the Revelation

I. **INTRODUCTION**

II. **SYSTEMS OF INTERPRETATION**

    A. Related to God

    B. Related to Scripture

    C. Related to Believers

    D. Premillennial System

    E. Postmillennial System

    F. Aumillennial Sysyem

III. **COMPARATIVE ANALYSIS OF GENESIS AND REVELATION**

    A. Creation

    B. Death

    C. Home

IV. **EVENTS LISTING**

V. **EVENTS GRAPHOC FORMULA**

LISTING OF EVENTS

    1. The Rapture of the Church

    2. The Judgment Seat of Christ (The First Judgment)

3. The Tribulation Period 7 years
4. The Battle of Armageddon
5. The Thousand Year Reign
6. Fire From Heaven
7. Satan cast into the lake of Fire
8. The Great White Throne Judgment (Second Judgment)
9. Heaven and Earth will pass away

REVELATION 1

VERSE BY VERSE

VERSE 1

The Revelation of Jesus Christ, which God gave until him, to show unto his servants things which must shortly come to pass; and he sent and signified <it> by his angel unto his servant John:

Revelation is the Greek word APOCALYPSES. It is composed from a preposition meaning "to take away" and it is taken from a verb meaning "to cover" therefore the meaning is to take away the cover. So the book of the Revelation is an unveiling.

Of Jesus Christ, of course we know that this book contains the Revelation of Jesus Christ this is not John's revelation it is Jesus Revelation. He who is Lord of All is able to look across all dispensations of time and give us His revelation.

God the Father is the source of this Revelation, He gave it to Jesus, His Son and now His Son is giving it to His servants. Things which must shortly come to past. The word shortly in the Greek is interesting in this text and it is written EN TACHEI it really conveys two ideas.

1. The idea of certainty.
2. The idea of a rapid time frame.

God's not saying that these things will happen in a matter of a few years, but He is saying when they start to happen, they will happen very quickly in rapid succession.

Sent and signified it. The word signified in the Greek ESEMANEN and it means to use symbols. We all know that words change meanings more than symbols do, so the Book of Revelation was written to describe events that would take place hundreds of years in the future and symbols were used to define truths.

By His angel under His servant John. The word angel is ANGELOS it means messenger.

VERSE 2
Who bare record of the word of God, and of the testimony of Jesus Christ, and of all things that he saw.

Who bare record of the Word of God and of the testimony of Jesus Christ, and of all things that He saw. This just simply means that He was a witness to this record.

The Blessed Terms

VERSE 3

Blessed <is> he that readeth, and they that hear the words of this prophecy, and keep those things which are written therein: for the time <is> at hand.

The word blessed means "Oh the Bliss!"

It would do us well to look at all the blessed terms seen in the Book of Revelation.

1. Blessed are those who read and obey the book
2. Blessed are the dead in Christ.
3. Blessed are those that keep their garments.
4. Blessed are those who are called to the marriage supper.
5. Blessed are those in the first resurrection.
6. Blessed are those who keep the sayings of His book.
7. Blessed are those who do His commandments.

The second thing this verse says is that the people need to hear with the intent of obeying.

Because the Bible says time is at hand. The words "At Hand" in the Greek is EGGUS. It means speed. In other words, the time will certainly come and it is rapidly approaching.

PICK-UP

VERSE 4

John to the seven churches which are in Asia: Grace <be> unto you, and peace, from his which is, and which was, and which is to come; and from the seven Spirits which are before his throne;

The number 7 refers to completion. There are many symbols used in the book of the Revelation. If you would like to read more about the importance of numbers in the Bible I suggest you read the book THEOMATICS by Lucas.

The 7 churches of course refers to 7 different dispensation time periods throughout the history of Christianity. The word "churches" is EKKLESIA in the Greek. It means "An Assembly or Those Who Are Called Out". Asia is the place where all 7 churches are located. "Grace be unto you and peace," is a common first century greeting. The idea in the original language for this common greeting with others is that you might have harmony in your relationships with others. When people would greet one another they would say, "may there be harmony in this relationship". The term "from him which is, and which was, and which is to come" is a reference to one word in the Greek and that is the word Jehovah. Jehovah is the name for God the Father, it means "Eternal

One". The terms 7 spirits which are before His throne is a reference to the Holy Spirit. 7 refers to the 7 attributes of the Holy Spirit.

VERSE 5
And from Jesus Christ, <who is> the faithful witness, <and> the first begotten of the dead, and the prince of the kings of the earth. Unto him that loved us, and washed us from our sins in his own blood,

The term "from Jesus Christ" is a picture of the complication of the trinity. This book is to the 7 churches in Asia and it is from the Father, Son and Holy Spirit. The reference to faithful witness, and Kings of the earth, deal with Jesus threefold aspect of His office, He is Prophet, Priest, and King. The verse goes on to tell us that Jesus has loved us; and the phrase, "in His own Blood", tells us that He has made a way for us to come into God's love, (Agape love in the Greek) and Jesus has cleansed us with His blood.

VERSE 6
And hath made us kings and priests unto God and his Father; to him <be> glory and dominion for ever and ever. Amen.

Verse 6 just simply says that Jesus is the one who received all the Glory and Honor and dominion forever. The word Glory in the Greek is "Doxa" and it refers to the fact that God should receive Glory because of His person. God is worthy to receive Glory forever.

VERSE 7

Behold, he cometh with clouds; and every eye shall see him, and they <also> which pierced him: and all kindreds of the earth shall wail because of him. Even so, Amen.

The phrase "He cometh with clouds" can be described as vehicles of God's supernatural power and deity. The phrase in this verse "every eye shall see him" is not a reference to the rapture of the church it is a reference to when Jesus comes back with His church to establish His Kingdom. The phrase, "they which also pierced him", is a reference to the nation Israel. The Bible says, they shall wail because of Him, they will mourn because they rejected Him as the Messiah.

The Deity of Jesus

VERSE 8

I am Alpha and Omega, the beginning and the ending, saith the Lord, which is, and which was, and which is to come, the Almighty.

Verse 8 we are given the attributes of the Deity of Jesus, He is Alpha and Omega, the first and last and this is in comparative analysis with the Greek alphabet since Alpha and Omega are the first and last letters of the Greek alphabet. In other words, Jesus is the sum total of everything that has existed from A to Z. He is omnipresent, He has always been; and He will be here when the end is over. He is ALL POWERFUL that is meant by the phrase, "the Almighty",

VERSE 9

I John, who also am your brother, and companion in tribulation, and in the kingdom and patience of Jesus Christ, was in isle that is called Patmos, for the word of God, and for the testimony of Jesus Christ.

John's phrase; "your brother and companion in tribulation", is a reference to the physical time in which he lived, Theologians believe that the book was written around AD 95. John was banished to the Isle of Patmos by Domitian. John was released eighteen months later after he had been on the Isle of Patmos by the emperor Nerva.

When John used the words Kingdom and patience of Jesus Christ, he was stating that he was the Christians' brother in the kingdom. If we are going to suffer together, then we are going to reign together. John was a witness for Jesus on the Isle of Patmos.

VERSE 10

I was in the Spirit on the Lord's Day, and heard behind me a great voice, as of a trumpet,

The phrase "in the Spirit" means that he was under the influence of the Holy Spirit and I believe that he was filled with the Holy Spirit. The phrase "on the Lord's Day" means that he received the vision on the first day of the week. The voice that sounded like "a trumpet" was the voice of Jesus.

Verse 11

Saying, I am Alpha and Omega, the first and the last: and, what thou seest, write in a book, and send <it> unto the seven churches which are in Asia; unto Ephesus, and unto Smyrna, and unto Pergamos, and unto Thyatira, and unto Sardis, and unto Philadelphia, and unto Laodicea.

Here again in this vision we see the attributes of Jesus that I have already mentioned concerning Him being the Alpha and the Omega. What you see, be sure you write it down and send it to the churches, The words; "what thou seest," is the Greek word BLEPO – it means to see with the physical eye.

Golden Candlesticks

VERSE 12

And I turned to see the voice that spoke with me. And being turned, I saw seven golden candlesticks;

There are a good many symbols in verse twelve, Seven is used to symbolize completion. Golden, I believe depicts righteousness and the words candlesticks literally means lampstands.

VERSE 13

And in the midst of the seven candlesticks <one> like unto the Son of man, clothed with a garment down to the foot, and girt about the paps with a golden girdle.

The phrase, "one like unto the Son of man" refers to God in His human form which is the incarnation and it was the title for the Messiah. The descriptive use of "the clothing of the garment down to the foot," means that this person is dressed like a king. The phrase gift about that paps means, "wrapped around the breasts" and of course the golden girdle is a picture of righteousness and it is more of an apron and it symbolizes service.

VERSE 14

His head and his hairs <were> white like wool, as white as snow; and his eyes <were> as a flame of fire;

The description of his head and his hair being white like wool stands for purity. It means that Jesus is eternal, He is the only sinless one. He is the ancient of days. The phrase "flame of fire" for His eyes means that His eyes can penetrate into the enter part of man. Jesus looks on the heart.

VERSE 15

And his feet like unto fine brass, as if they burned in a furnace; and his voice as the sound of many waters.

The phrase, "His feet like unto fine brass, as if they burned in a furnace", the feet symbolize a foundation, the brass as always is a picture of judgment. The phrase, "His voice as the sound of many waters, "symbolizes strength and power the mighty power of His Word.

Seven Stars

VERSE 16

And he had in his right hand seven stars: and out of his mouth went a sharp two-edged sword: and his countenance <was> as the sun shineth in his strength.

The seven stars symbolize the messengers or pastors of the seven churches that He is writing to. "Out of His mouth went a sharp two-edged sword," refers to the penetrating and convicting power of the Word of Christ. I believe there is a life and death in the Words of Christ. By that I mean He can speak and promote life and He speaks and there will be death. An indication of this is seen in one of the last great battles of this planet in the Book of the Revelation when Jesus speaks and millions of people fall dead, The Battle of Armageddon. The Bible says His countenance was as the sunshine. This deals with Jesus being the Light of Heaven, Malachi called Jesus, "the Son of Righteousness".

VERSE 17

And when I saw him, I fell at his feet as dead. And he laid his right hand upon me, saying unto me, Fear not; I am the first and the last:

When John saw Jesus this way he fainted. Then you see the words, "fear not". We should not live in the realm of fear but in the realm of Faith. Fear is the opposite if Faith.

Power over Hell

VERSE 18

I <am> he that liveth, and was dead; and, behold, I am alive for evermore, Amen; and have the keys of hell and of death.

Jesus is stating that He is alive and He has conquered death and He has access and authority over death itself. The phrase "hell" in this passage really means Hades, it is the Old Testament word for Sheol, Sheol is the paradise side of Hell where Old Testament Saints went until Jesus died on the Cross. Once Jesus died on the cross and paid our sin debt for all generations past, present and future then Jesus descended into hell and took all the Old Testament Saints captive who were in the paradise side of Sheol and carried them to His Heavenly Father in Heaven and rushed back to appear before Mary in the garden on Easter Sunday morning. So we know that Jesus has the power over death and hell.

VERSE 19

Write the things which thou hast seen, and the things which are, and the things which shall be hereafter;

This Revelation is to John, but it is being told by Jesus Christ. The best outline for the book of the Revelation is found in this verse.

1. The things which thou hast seen.
2. The things which are.
3. The things which shall be hereafter.

VERSE 20

The mystery of the seven stars which thou sawest in my right hand, and the seven golden candlesticks. The seven stars are the angels of the seven churches: and the seven candlesticks which thou sawest are the seven churches.

The word mystery is MUSTERION in the Greek. It refers to truth that will never be discerned or understood by human wisdom. God gives it by direct Revelation. The seven stars are the angels, and the word angel actually means "messenger". The seven golden candlesticks are in reference to the churches.

VERSE BY VERSE

VERSE 1

Unto the angel of the church of Ephesus write; These things saith he that holdeth the seven stars in his right hand, who walketh in the midst of the seven golden candlesticks;

The word "angel" means "messenger" and refers to the pastor. The word "Ephesus" means "desired". This church represents the church age from AD 30 to AD 100. The word "holdeth" means "to grip" the seven stars are the seven pastors, the seven golden candlesticks are the seven churches.

VERSE 2

I know thy works, and your labor and thy patience, and how thou canst not bear them which are evil: and thou hast tried them which say they are apostles, and are not, and hast found them liars:

When Jesus says, "I know" the Greek word there is "OIDA which means to have fullness of knowledge", so Jesus is telling the church that He knows their works, their labor, their patience and the fact that the church does not support those who are evil. He states that "they have tried them which say that they are apostles and are not". This is a reference to the fact that many first century folks claim to be apostles but they were not of course. An apostle is one that must have seen Jesus personally. His phrase "found them liars" means that "he has inquired and they are found to be false".

VERSE 3

And hast borne, and hast patience, and for my name's sake hast labored, and hast not fainted.

The phrase "hast borne, and hast not fainted" means that "they stayed in the battle and they remain faithful to Jesus in the midst of the battle".

VERSE 4

Nevertheless I have <somewhat> against thee, because thou hast left thy first love.

Jesus is stating "that something is wrong with the church they have left their first love, they've been so busy defending their faith and fighting evil that they neglected their relationship with Jesus". There are many churches today that are fighting for good causes but they are not lifting up the person of Jesus. In other words their motives were wrong.

VERSE 5

Remember therefore from whence thou art fallen, and repent, and do the first works; or else I will come unto thee quickly, and will remove thy candlestick out of his place, except thou repent.

Jesus advise to them was to "remember their relationship to Him and to turn from their sin, to repent". The word "repent" in the Greek is "METANOEO" and it means, "to turn around completely". Jesus is calling him to do the first works which is to love Him first and He will lead you into everything else you need to do: Prayer, Bible study, Church Attendance, Witnessing, and so on. His phrase that "if you don't do what I'm asking you to do means that He will not be in our worship, He will come and remove the candlestick". There must be repentance or Jesus will take His working power and His presence out of all that we do. I believe that a church can sin collectively as a group against God and quench the working power of the Holy Spirit of God.

Nicolaitanes

VERSE 6

But this thou hast, that thou hatest the deeds of the Nicolaitanes, which I also hate.

The "Nicolaitanes" reference to this verse or group of people who were in the church government who had the power to select the priesthood and Jesus said that He hated them. This is a picture of Political Turf Shepherds today in the church who throw a fit when they don't get their way.

VERSE 7

He that hath an ear, let him hear what the Spirit saith unto the churches; To him that overcometh will I give to eat of the tree of life, which is in the midst of the paradise of God.

The Message to the church at Ephesus is the fact that Jesus just wants us to love Him and wanted them to love him. If you repent and return to Jesus then you will overcome.

VERSE 8

And unto the angel of the church in Smyrna write; These things saith the first and the last, which was dead, and is alive;

The word "angel" means "messenger", "Smyrna" means "MYRRH" this was a pain killer and was also used as embalming fluid. Jesus is stating this phrase that "He is the Eternal One". Reminding us of who He is and His attributes.

VERSE 9

I know thy works, and tribulation, and poverty, (but thou art rich) and <I know> the blasphemy of them which say they are Jews, and are not, but <are> the synagogue of Satan.

The word "tribulation" in this verse means "to be under pressure" and the word "poverty" means "a beggar or one who is destitute". The Jews in Smyrna were more hostile to Christians than most places, they had slandered them. Jesus is just stating "that a true Jew is one that had been born again through Jesus Christ". The synagogue of Satan is a reference to where the Jews met to worship God.

VERSE 10

Fear none of those things which thou shalt suffer: behold, the devil shall cast <some> of you into prison, that ye may be tried; and ye shall have tribulation ten days: be thou faithful unto death, and I will give thee a crown of life.

Jesus is dealing with the idea here that fear and faith cannot coexist together. He talks about what will happen with Satan and the fact that Satan hates God and he hates God's people. Satan is the real cause of all the problems in the church. That is still true today. The phrase "ten days" "tribulation" is a reference to a complete period of time, or it could be a reference to the ten rulers who rule during this church age from about AD100 to AD300". Jesus talking about "being faithful unto death is a mandate for all of those in the church". Church history tells us that POLYCARP was the godly pastor at Smyrna who was burned to death at the age of 86.

VERSE 11
He that hath an ear, let him hear what the Spirit saith unto the churches; He that overcometh shall not be hurt of the second death.

The message to the church was to be faithful to Jesus even if it cost you, your life; and to hear what He is saying to you. If you do this you are not going to suffer this second death which is eternal damnation in a Lake of Fire which burns forever and ever.

VERSE 12
And to the angel of the church in Pergamos write; These things saith he which hath the sharp sword with two edges;

Pergamos comes from two Greek words, the Greek word "GAMOS" which means "married" and the Greek word "PER" meaning "evil". So the church was married to the world. Jesus talks about the "sharp sword with two edges.

This is a reference to the fact that the sword is the Word of God, and the Word of God always reveals Truth".

First Martyr

VERSE 13

I know thy works and where thou dwellest, <even> where Satan's seat <is>: and thou holdest fast my name, and hast not denied my faith, even in those days wherein Antipas <was> my faithful martyr, who was slain among you, where Satan dwelleth.

Again we see this phrase "I know thy works", it means "to know in full". When Jesus talks about "to know where they dwell, He is dealing with a permanent dwelling". Pergamos was a Roman town that had a medical library of over two-hundred thousand volumes and had a large concentration of Paganism, Demon worship, idolatry and evil. Jesus thanks them, because they have lived up to His name and they are Holy and sperate unto Him. The word "Antipas" is a reference to "the first Christian martyr killed by the Romans according to secular history, he was in this church". We know that Stephen was the first Christian martyr killed by the Jews. But Antipas was the first

Christian martyr killed by the Romans. The word "martyr" means "witness".

VERSE 14
But I have a few things against thee, because thou hast there them that hold the doctrine of Balaam, who taught Balac to cast a stumbling block before the children of Israel, to eat things sacrificed unto idols, and to commit fornication.

Jesus is dealing with the doctrine of Balaam which is found in Numbers 21-31. "Balaam" means "the introduction of Paganism among God's children". What persecution could not do in that church, Paganism did.

VERSE 15
So hast thou also them that hold the doctrine of the Nicolaitanes, which thing I hate.

Again there is a reference to the "Nicolaitanes", as we have stated previously "combination of the Nicolaitanes and Salaam the practice of worldliness a priesthood rolling over people". Jesus said, He hated these practices.

VERSE 16
Repent; or else I will come unto thee quickly, and will fight against them with the sword of my mouth.

He tells them "to repent". He means that "they need to turn around from these false doctrines or else He will fight them with this truth, meaning the word of His truth".

VERSE 17

He that hath an ear, let him hear what the Spirit saith unto the churches; To him that overcometh will I give to eat of the hidden manna, and will give him a white stone, and in the stone a new name written, which no man knoweth saving he that receiveth <it>.

Jesus is saying be sure you reject false doctrines and I will give you the promise of being an overcomer. The reference to hidden manna is a fact that Jesus is the hidden manna.

Reference to a "white stone" is the fact "that we have God's guidance to lead us today in a difficult time". We have the Holy Spirit to lead us. The High Priest in Israel wore a white stone on his breast plate, this is a diamond. Reference to "a new name written" can be compared to the name of God has seen in the stone that was worn by the Priest.

VERSE 18

And unto the angel of the church in Thyatira write; These things saith the Son of God, who hath his eyes like unto a flame of fire, and his feet <are> like fine brass;

"Thyatira" is a word formed from two words meaning "a sacrifice or an offering". In this verse "Jesus represents Himself as the Son of God. We also see another picture that we have previously seen in His description to the seven churches concerning His eyes and His feet".

VERSE 19

I know thy works, and charity, and service, and faith, and thy patience, and thy works; and the last <to be> more than the first.

Again we see Jesus using the phrase "I know, He knows about their works, their charity, their service, and their faith and their patience".

VERSE 20

Notwithstanding I have a few things against thee, because thou sufferest that woman Jezebel, which calleth herself a prophetess, to teach and to seduce my servants to commit fornication, and to eat things sacrificed unto idols.

The word "sufferest" means "to allow". The reference to that "woman" can either be a reference to a woman or a wife". "The name Jezebel is the name that we have seen in the Old Testament". There are several suggestions as to who this lady is. She is referred to the one in the Old Testament, or some say that it was Lydia in the New Testament; but no one knows for sure. It is a strong possibility that this is a reference to a pastor's wife who was bringing false doctrine to the church, and Jesus detested her works, the work of wickedness. She is compared, I believe, to the Jezebel of the Old Testament. She was the wife of Ahab, she was the woman who introduced Paganism, into worship. Jesus says here that she calls herself a "prophetess" which means she has a message from God, but she is just teaching the people to do evil practices and to commit physical fornication and to go against all of the law concerning sacrifices.

VERSE 21

"And I gave her time to repent of her sexual immorality, and she did not repent.

Jesus is just saying that, He is giving her time to repent but that she would rather have the judgment of God.

VERSE 22

"Indeed I will cast her into a sickbed, and those who commit adultery with her into great tribulation, unless they repent of their deeds.

He will throw her violently into a bed. The word for bed in the Greek is "KLINE", which means a bed of suffering.

Those who commit adultery with her will be in great tribulation, however this is not a reference to the great tribulation after the rapture of the church but it's a reference to the present time of great suffering. It is a picture of the dark ages.

VERSE 23

"I will kill her children with death, and all the churches shall know that I am He who searches the minds and hearts. And I will give to each one of you according to your works.

The phrase "I will strike her children dead" and "the church will have the testimony of God's justice and judgment is a powerful demonstration". Jesus says "He searches the hearts, "He searches the seed of emotions" and of course He knows about our works.

VERSE 24

"Now to you I say, and to the rest in Thyatira, as many as do not have this doctrine, who have not known the depths of Satan, as they say, I will put on you no other burden.

Jesus is stating in this verse God always has a Remnant in every church. There is no thing that God does not know. He shows His mercy here when He says that, "I will put on you no other burden".

VERSE 25

"But hold fast what you have till I come.

Hold fast means to "grip tightly", to "stand fast" till I come.

VERSE 26

"And he who overcomes, and keeps My works until the end, to him I will give power over the nations;

The dream of this church is to be a powerful institution that rules the world and Jesus is just stating that, "I will give power to the true church in my Kingdom".

VERSE 27

'He shall rule them with a rod of iron; They shall be dashed to pieces like the potter's vessels'; as I also have received from My Father;

This is a quote of Psalm 2:8-9, and it refers to "Jesus' rule through the millennial reign".

Morning Star

VERSE 28

And I will give him the morning star.

"Morning Star" is a reference to "Jesus in Revelation 22:16". I think this is a reference to the Second Coming; at the darkest hour Jesus will come.

VERSE 29

He that hath an ear, let him hear what the Spirit saith unto the churches.

"Let the Spirit saith unto the churches" the message is to "remain true to Jesus and you will reign with Him".

REVELATION 3

VERSE 1

And unto the angel of the church in Sardis write; These things saith he that hath the seven Spirits of God, and the seven stars; I know thy works, that thou hast a name that thou livest, and art dead.

The phrase "these things saith he" is a reference to "Jesus and is taken from chapter 1". "Seven Spirits of God". This is a reference to the fullness of the Holy Spirit and not a reference to seven different spirits. "The seven stars". This refers to the messengers or pastors of the churches that are being addressed. When Jesus says "I know thy works" it means "he has full knowledge of or knows them in an intimate way". The phrase "thou hast a name that thou livest, and art dead". This deals with the reputation of the church at Sardis, the reputation was that it was alive but in reality it was really dead; they had a form of godliness but denied the power thereof. This is a picture of a cold, formal, highly organized church that lacks the warmth that only the Holy Spirit of God can bring in worship.

VERSE 2

Be watchful, and strengthen the things which remain, that are ready to die: for I have not found thy works perfect before God.

"Be Watchful" This is a strong word that means to arouse yourself, in other words, He is telling the church to wake up. Strengthen the things that remain. The word strengthen here means to make fast or to establish. There was a remnant of the true church that remained in the church and God always has a remnant. They needed to strengthen, establish, and make fast the things that they have already learned in His Word. "That are ready to die", this word "ready" in the Greek is the word "MELLO" it means to "be about to". So what Jesus is saying here is to tell them to strengthen their faith because some of the members of the church were about to die and to be persecuted and they needed to be ready. "For I have not found thy works perfect". The word perfect is the same word "filled", that Paul uses in Ephesians 5:18 it means to fill or be full. The problem was that the church at Sardis was working but they working in the flesh, they were not filled with the Holy Spirit. "Before God". This phrase means; what matters most of all in all of our churches is not what we think, and not what we think people know, but what God knows! That is what matters.

Hold Fast

VERSE 3

Remember therefore how thou hast received and heard, and hold fast, and repent. If therefore thou shalt not watch, I will come on thee as a thief, and thou shalt not know what hour I will come upon thee.

"Remember therefore how thou hast received and heard". The Holy Spirit is asking these men to remember and bring unto repentance, the early days when they heard the Word of God and received it. "Hold fast and repent" the phrase "hold fast" in the Greek is "PEERED" and it means to watch over or "to guard". We need to guard our relationship with Jesus and our fellowshipping with Jesus. Stay as close to Jesus as we possibly can. "If therefore thou shalt not watch" this means if you do awake yourself God's judgment will come. The phase "I will come on thee as a thief, and thou shalt not know what hour I will come upon thee" means that Jesus is just stating; if you do not wake up my coming is going to be so sudden and unexpected to you that you are not going to be ready.

VERSE 4

Thou hast a few names even in Sardis which have not defiled their garments; and they shall walk with me in white: for they are worthy.

"Thou halt a few names even in Sardis" this just means that God is still in control of the church and there is always a remnant in the church. Many theologians believe that this is the picture of the church age where the Protestant movement began out of Catholicism. "Which have not defiled their garments" garments refer to their lifestyle or the way that they lived. "They shall walk with me in white" white represents purity and holiness and of course to "walk with God" implies fellowship. "For they are worthy" this is a borrowed worthiness because none of us are worthy in the power of our own selves.

Romans 3:10

As it is written, There is none righteous, no, not one:

VERSE 5

He that overcometh, the same shall be clothed in white raiment; and I will not blot out his name out of the book of life, but I will confess his name before my Father, and before his angels.

"He that overcometh" the overcomer in the New Testament was the person that has been born again. "The same shall be clothed in white raiment" these are the ones who are truly clothed in the righteousness of Jesus and we will be declared just on the Day of Judgment. "I will not blot out his name out of the Book of Life" this is not a threat it is a promise, those who have been born again have their names written in the Lambs Book of Life and those who do not have their names written in the Lambs Book of Life at the end of time will be cast into Hell will have their names blotted out of the Book of Life. "But I will confess His name before my Father, and before his angels". The word confess in the Greek is "HOMOLOGEO" it means to speak the same thing. The word "profess" is the same word as the word confess in our text. There is coming a day when Jesus will profess and confess that you are a son or a daughter of God, that you belong to Him, that you have been born again.

VERSE 6

He that hath an ear, let him hear what the Spirit saith unto the churches.

"Hear what the Spirit saith unto the churches" this just simply means the message to the church of Sardis means that they need to get away from reputation and look at reality.

VERSE 7

And to the angel of the church in Philadelphia write; These things saith he that is holy, he that is true, he that hath the key of David, he that openeth, and no man shutteth; and shutteth, and no man openeth;

"Philadelphia" the word Philadelphia is composed of the words "Phileo" meaning love and "Adelphos" meaning brother. So of course the word means brotherly love. The phrase "He that is Holy", the word Holy is "HAGIOS" it means set apart. This is Jesus title it also refers to his character. "He that is true", the word for true is "ALEATHINOS" denotes a sense of what is genuine. "Hath the key of David" this just says that Jesus is the key of David in the fact that He is opening all the treasures of God and no one can get to God unless they come through Jesus Christ. "He that openeth and no man shutteth" Jesus is the one that has all the power and He is the one that opens and closes doors for the church. When Jesus opens the door, no man can shut it, when He closes the door, no man can open it.

VERSE 8

I know thy works: behold, I have set before thee an open door, and no man can shut it: for thou hast a little strength, and hast kept my word, and hast not denied my name.

"I have set before thee an open door" literal meaning of this text is I have given you a door which I myself have already opened for you. So there was a big door of opportunity for the church here at Philadelphia for witnessing.

"And no man can shut it", this means that you cannot curse what God has blessed. The phrase "thou hast a little strength" Jesus is stating here that the strength of the church at Philadelphia was there weakness. The secret of accomplishing great things for God is not in our own strength but a reliance of His own strength. "Hast kept my word" this simple means being obedient to His Word. The phase "Hast not denied my name" Jesus' name means Savior; and these folks needed to live Holy lives and recognize before people around them that they belonged to Jesus.

VERSE 9

Behold , I will make them of the synagogue of Satan, which say they are Jews, and are not, but do lie; behold, I will make them to come and worship before thy feet, and to know that I have loved thee.

The word "Behold" in verse nine means "to see" and the phrase "I will make them of the synagogue of Satan" is a reference to the place where the Jews worshipped God. Jesus goes on to say that a true Jew is one that has been born again through Jesus Christ. The phrase here "but do lie", means that they are false. The phrase "I will make them to come and worship before thy feet" means that God will vindicate His people. The phrase; "and to know that I have loved thee" speaks of the great depth of God's love.

VERSE 10

Because thou hast kept the word of my patience, I also will keep thee from the hour of temptation, which shall come upon all the world, to try them that dwell upon the earth.

"Because thou hast kept the word of my patience" a literal translation here is; that thou hast kept my word with patience and so this church was obedient to God's word. Jesus said "I will also keep thee" meaning I will preserve thee. Preserve thee from the hour of temptation the word "Hour" denotes a period or a season; and the word "Temptation" denotes what is permitted or sent to them. This is a reference to the great tribulation that will last seven years after the rapture of the church. The phrase "which shall come upon all the world", the word for world here refers to the inhabited earth not the physical one. Even though the physical earth will be affected, the purpose of the Tribulation itself is to bring judgment on the inhabitants of the earth and not the earth itself.

VERSE 11

Behold , I come quickly: hold that fast with what you have, that no man take thy crown.

"Behold, I come quickly" this is the key note of the book. "Hold that fast which thou hast" "Hold fast" means to be strong, mighty, to prevail. It is the idea to be stronger than your opponent. The phrase "no man take thy crown" means that when you have a victor's crown awarded to you for winning the race, do not let others still your awards, this is not a reference to our salvation.

VERSE 12

Him that overcometh will I make a pillar in the temple of my God, and he shall go no more out: and I will write upon him the name of my God, and the name of the city of my God, <which is> new Jerusalem, which cometh down out of heaven from my God: and <I will write upon him> my new name.

We see this phrase all through the Bible in the Book of the Revelation "to him that overcometh". Jesus says; "Will I make a pillar in the temple of my God" the word pillar means supporting structure. In Philadelphia there was a public temple where an individual could leave a legacy for himself by having a pillar erected with his name inscribed on it. Jesus says those who serve him will be a pillar in the Eternal Temple of God. The phrase "he shall go no more out" is one of separation, it means that there will be no separation in heaven, we will never have to say goodbye. The phrase "I will write upon him the name of my God" this is simply a sign of ownership, we are God's possession. The phrase "and the name of my city of my God" this is a sign of citizenship. Our citizenship is not of this world, but of Heaven. The phrase which is New Jerusalem means it is new in a sense of quality, former nature, of course Jerusalem is the capital city of God's people. One day we will dwell in the New Jerusalem. The phrase "I will write upon him my new name" literally means, "I'm going to give him my own name".

VERSE 13

He that hath an ear, let him hear what the Spirit saith unto the churches.

"He that hath an ear, let him hear" of course this is the same phrase we've heard before and it just means to have spiritual discernment as to what God is saying.

VERSE 14

And unto the angel of the church of the Laodiceans write; These things saith the Amen, the faithful and true witness, the beginning of the creation of God;

"The church of the Laodiceans" was a church ruled by the people and not by the Lord Jesus. The phrase "these things saith the Amen"; this is taken from God's description of the Lord Jesus; and the word "Amen" means "so let it be". Jesus is the Truth. The word for Truth is the Hebrew word for "Amen". "The faithful and true witness" refers to the fact that Jesus is not only the Truth, but He is the only True Witness". The phrase "the beginning of the creation of God", The word "beginning" means that Jesus is the source of everything that was created.

VERSE 15

I know thy works, that thou art neither cold nor hot: I would thou wert cold or hot.

"I know thy works"; this means to know in full, to intimately know. The phrase "thou art neither cold nor hot" deals with growing cold. Apparently the church at Laodicea had at one time been on fire for Jesus and they were boiling hot and now they were growing cold. Jesus said, "I would thou wert cold or hot" so it is Jesus' desire that we be one way or the other for him. Nothing is more heartbreaking to Jesus than a luke warm church.

VERSE 16

So then because thou art lukewarm, and neither cold nor hot, I will spue thee out of my mouth.

The phrase "so then because thou art lukewarm, and neither cold nor hot", the word "lukewarm" in the Greek is "Chliaros", and it means tepid or warm. It's like drinking warm water, it is nauseating and makes you want to spit it out of your mouth and that is what he is talking about in this text. "To spue" really means; "to vomit with extreme discuss".

VERSE 17

Because thou sayest, I am rich, and increased with goods, and have need of nothing; and knowest not that thou art wretched, and miserable, and poor, and blind, and naked:

"Because thou sayest, I am rich, and have need of nothing". The church had so much pride they couldn't see what they needed they were looking at material things instead of spiritual truths and treasures. Not only were they complacent, indifferent and proud but they were ignorant, they did not know what to look, they did not know what the spiritual virtues were. The phrase "thou art wretched" is an old adjective, meaning to endure a burden, it means someone who is callous. Each one of these descriptive terms are powerful in this verse. The word "miserable" means to be "pitied", the word "poor" means a "beggar", the word "blind" means "spiritual blindness", the word "naked" which means Jesus saw them as they actually were.

Tried in the Fire

VERSE 18

I counsel thee to buy of me gold tried in the fire, that thou mayest be rich; and white raiment, that thou mayest be clothed, and <that> the shame of thy nakedness do not appear; and anoint thine eyes with eyesalve, that thou mayest see.

"I counsel you to buy from Me", Jesus is saying the true riches come from God. The word "gold" means "riches". "Tried in the fire", refers to spiritual gold that has been put to the test. "White raiment, that thou mayest be clothed", we need to be clothed in the beauty of God's holiness and we also need to see what God sees, when Jesus opens our eyes, when He uses eyesalve we will be able to see what He sees.

VERSE 19
As many as I love, I rebuke and chasten: be zealous therefore, and repent.

"As many as I love, I rebuke and chasten" the word for "chasten" is "Paideuo" and it actually means to train a child, it means gentle instruction. The words "be zealous" and "repent" the word "zealous" in the Greek is "Zelos" which means to boil. Jesus says reach your boiling point and get on fire for me and repent.

VERSE 20
Behold , I stand at the door, and knock: if any man hear my voice, and open the door, I will come in to him, and will sup with him, and he with me.

"Behold, I stand at the door, and knock" many preachers use this as an evangelistic verse but this is not written as an evangelistic verse it is written to the church. One of the saddest pictures in the New Testament is the fact that Jesus is knocking at the door of this church and they will not let him in. The invitation is extended to anyone within the church. The phrase "will sup with him, and he with me" refers to the chief meal of the day, it means I will have the chief meal of the day with you.

VERSE 21

To him that overcometh will I grant to sit with me in my throne, even as I also overcame, and am set down with my Father in his throne.

"I will grant to sit with me in my throne" this is something that happens to the person who is the overcomer.

VERSE 22

He that hath an ear, let him hear what the Spirit saith unto the churches.

"Hear the Spirit saith unto the churches" message to the church in Laodecia is the church that pleases Jesus is the one that is on fire for Him, anything else Him sick.

INTRODUCTION TO CHAPTER FOUR REVELATION

I. **THE SUMMONS FROM THE THRONE 4:1**

A. EVIDENCE OF THE CHURCH "CAUGHT UP"

B. SUDDEN EVENT

C. DOORS OF REVELATION

1. DOOR OF SERVICE 3:8

2. DOOR CLOSED 3:20

3. DOOR INTO HEAVEN 4:1

4. DOOR OUT FROM HEAVEN 19:11

II. **GLORY OF THE THRONE 4:2-3**

A. GEMS OF GOD TO SYMBOLIZE HIS GLORY

B. RAINBOW GOD'S PROMISE, A COVENANT OF MERCY

III. **ELDERS AROUND THE THRONE 4:4**

A. THEY ARE NOT ANGELS

B. ROYAL REDEEMED

IV. THOSE BEFORE THE THRONE

A. LAMPS

B. SEA OF GLASS

C. LIVING CREATURES

REVELATION 4

VERSE 1

After this I looked, and, behold, a door <was> opened in heaven: and the first voice which I heard <was> as it were of a trumpet talking with me; which said, Come up hither, and I will show thee things which must be hereafter.

The phrase "after this" in verse one simply is a phrase that means that the division of the church age is ended. The phrase "a door was opened in heaven" allows John to look into Heaven and see that Jesus is the door. The phrase "the first voice which I heard as it were of a trumpet", the trumpet was always used to get the attention of the people and to make a proclamation. Of course this is a picture of the rapture of the church. The phrase "come up, hither, and I will show thee things which must be hereafter" the scene is changing now from earth to Heaven and John has been given a picture of the church age and he is about to see what is going to happen when all of that is concluded. The awesome period of great tribulation is coming and it is necessary because of man's rebellion against God. Before it comes, the church will be taken from the earth, so John's "rapture", (which is a Latin word, meaning to taken away suddenly), symbolizes the churches Rapture.

VERSE 2

And immediately I was in the spirit; and, behold, a throne was set in heaven, and <one> sat on the throne.

The phrase "I was in the spirit" John was already in the Spirit, but now he receives a fresh outpouring of the grace of God. The phrase "a throne was set in heaven" John is just stating that the throne had a great foundation, a throne that has been long established by God who is the ruler of the Universe. The phrase "the one who sat on the throne" literally reads in the Greek "on the throne a sitting one".

Half Bow Rainbow

VERSE 3

And he that sat was to look upon like a jasper and a sardine stone: and <there was> a rainbow round about the throne, in sight like unto an emerald.

"He that sat was to look upon like a jasper and a sardine stone" Jasper was the last stone on the High Priest breastplate, so Jasper refers to a modern stone that we know is clear as crystal, this is a diamond. The sardine stone was the first stone on the High Priest's Breastplate.

The sardine stone is blood red and so this refers to the sacrifice that Jesus made for our sins. The Bible says "there was a rainbow around about the throne like unto an emerald". This was not a regular rainbow, but a half bow that is a multicolored rainbow. It is green and it is one circle. It is a complete circle above the throne. The green color denotes that which is living and it denotes the fact that God has made a covenant to give us eternal life.

Twenty Four Elders

VERSE 4

And round about the throne <were> four and twenty seats: and upon the seats I saw four and twenty elders sitting, clothed in white raiment; and they had on their heads crowns of gold.

The phrase "round about the throne were four and twenty seats" there were twenty-four thrones around God's throne and these were seats of authority. This is a picture of the twenty-four elders. The name elder is never applied to angels in the Bible. Angels do not wear crowns and angels do not sit on thrones. These elders have been granted authority and they are rulers, they are clothed in white raiment which means that they have been redeemed by Jesus and they are wearing crowns meaning that this is a victor's crown, these are really the redeemed of God. These twenty-four elders in Heaven seem to represent all those who have been redeemed throughout the ages. In the New Jerusalem the twelve gates of the city are named after the twelve sons of Jacob and the twelve foundations on which the city wall is built after the twelve apostles of Jesus. So the twelve apostles represent the New Testament Saints and the twelve sons of Jacob represent the Old Testament Saints and the two groups together adds up to twenty-four and this is representative of all the redeemed of all the ages.

VERSE 5

And out of the throne proceeded lightnings and thundering and voices: and <there were> seven lamps of fire burning before the throne, which are the seven Spirits of God.

The phrase "and out of the throne proceeded lightnings and thundering and voices" - Thunderstorms are often used to portray God's divine power and His judgments with the picture of the fact that God is Holy. The phrase "there were seven lamps of fire burning before the throne" fire is often used in the Bible as a symbol of judgment, seven is referred to that which is complete. I believe that the fullness of God's judgment is complete in that it is about to be unleashed on the earth. The phrase "which are the seven Spirits of God" the Holy Spirit is referred to in this manner. He is called the Spirit of the Lord, the Spirit of Wisdom, the Spirit of Understanding, the Spirit of Counsel, the Spirit of Might, the Spirit of Knowledge, the Spirit of the Fear of the Lord, God uses the Holy Spirit to bring men to repentance.

VERSE 6

And before the throne <there was> a sea of glass like unto crystal: and in the midst of the throne, and round about the throne, <were> four beasts full of eyes before and behind.

"Before the throne there was a sea of glass", there was no need for continual cleansing in Heaven for we are made clean with the blood of Jesus Christ and so there is a sea of glass which looks like crystal. The word here in the Greek is really "Krustallos" which means ice and it emphasize that there is no longer a need for the cleansing of water, because we have been washed in the blood. The phrase "in the midst of the throne, and round about the throne" tells us there are four sides of the throne. The phrase "four beast" is a picture of the living creatures. Ezekiel describes these living creatures, they are responsible for guarding God's Holiness.

This <is> the living creature that I saw under the God of Israel by the river of Chebar; and I knew that they <were> the cherubims.

The phrase "full of eyes before and behind" refers to the fact that the four beast can see and they can perceive and they are intelligent. They know about past, present and future.

VERSE 7

And the first beast <was> like a lion, and the second beast like a calf, and the third beast had a face as a man, and the fourth beast <was> like a flying eagle.

The phrase "the first beast was like a lion" the lion is the King of the Jungle and here it represents the majesty and strength of the angelic creature. The phrase "the second beast is like a calf", this is the same Greek word used for the word ox, it means an animal of which is a servant. "The third beast had a face as a man" of course man is the most intelligent of all God's creatures. "The fourth beast was like a flying eagle" a flying eagle sores to great heights. This beast was capable of executing God's will very swiftly.

Four Beasts

VERSE 8

And the four beasts had each of them six wings about
<him>; and <they were> full of eyes within: and they rest
not day and night, saying, Holy, holy, holy, Lord God
Almighty, which was, and is, and is to come.

"The four beasts had each of them six wings about him" the
Bible says in Isaiah 6:2 that they had six wings, two of them
covered his face, signifying reverence for God, two covered
his feet signifying modesty and humility, and two helped him
to fly signifying swift to carry out God's will. Here again in
verse 8 they were full of eyes within this means they had the
ability to see and intelligence and they did not rest day or
night. They were not given intermission from their labor.
These four creatures were saying "Holy, Holy, Holy", of
course I believe that the repetition of the word Holy, Holy,
Holy means God the Father is Holy, God the Son is Holy,
and God the Holy Spirit is Holy. The term "Lord God
Almighty" means Emperor or King. The word God means
Deity. This is an exclusive title for God only.

VERSE 9

And when those beasts give glory and honor and thanks to him that sat on the throne, who liveth for ever and ever,

"When those beasts give glory and honor and thanks" the four creatures lead in a chorus in Praise to God. He that sat on the throne is the triune God and the phrase literally means; "who liveth forever and forever". The fact that He lives unto the ages of the ages.

VERSE 10

The four and twenty elders fall down before him that sat on the throne, and worship him that liveth for ever and ever, and cast their crowns before the throne, saying,

"The four and twenty elders fall down and worship him" this is the redeemed of all the ages. And the four angelic creatures praise God and they join in with the four and twenty elders who cast their crowns before Him and this is a glorious climax of their praise. The twenty-four elders cast in their victor's crowns at the feet of Jesus who is the Holy victor.

VERSE 11

Thou art worthy, 0 Lord, to receive glory and honor and power: for thou hast created all things, and for thy pleasure they are and were created.

They began to worship saying that God is worthy of praise and that He will receive praise because He created all things. This means that God is the source of all that ever was, that ever is, and that ever shall be. The phrase "for thy pleasure they are and were created" literally means, "because of your will everything exists and is created".

REVELATION 5

VERSE 1

And I saw in the right hand of him that sat on the throne a book written within and on the backside, sealed with seven seals.

The phrase "in the right hand of him that sat on the throne" literally means "upon the right hand". The sealed book that John saw was in the palm of God's right hand. The phrase "a book written within and on the backside" really means that this book is a scroll, it was written on the front and the back. "The Seven seals" on the scroll represent the fact that it was top secret.

VERSE 2

And I saw a strong angel proclaiming with a loud voice, Who is worthy to open the book, and to loose the seals thereof?

The phrase "I saw a strong angel" this angel may *be* Gabriel because in the book of Daniel, he was instructed to seal up the prophecy of the book and here he is announcing that the same prophecy is ready to be revealed. He proclaims with a loud voice and he is heard throughout heaven.

VERSE 3

And no man in heaven, nor in earth, neither under the earth, was able to open the book, neither to look thereon

The phrase "And no man in heaven," literally means no one in heaven has the right. The phrase "nor in earth," means that no one on the earth has the right to open the book and the phrase "neither under the earth," is a reference to the fact that the Old Testament Saints in the paradise side of Sheol do not have the right to open the book. Neither do any demons or the Devil himself have the right.

VERSE 4

And I wept much, because no man was found worthy to open and to read the book, neither to look thereon.

The phrase "And I wept much," means I kept on weeping much. John's weeping was hysterical; because no one could open the book. No man was found worthy.

Root of David

VERSE 5

And one of the elders saith unto me, Weep not: behold, the Lion of the tribe of Judah, the Root of David, hath prevailed to open the book, and to loose the seven seals thereof.

"And one of the elders saith unto me," one of the twenty-four elders described in Revelation chapter 4 approached John with a word of encouragement; Don't weep, behold the "Lion of the tribe of Judah" is "The Root of David". The title "Lion of the tribe of Judah" is taken from Genesis 49, it is a reference to Jesus. Hebrews 7:14 the title "The Root of David" is a reference to Jesus and Isaiah 11:10, Romans 15:12 says that Jesus has prevailed, that He has already conquered! There is only one that is worthy to open the book, Jesus is Lord!

VERSE 6

And I beheld, and, lo, in the midst of the throne and of the four beasts, and in the midst of the elders, stood a Lamb as it had been slain, having seven horns and seven eyes, which are the seven Spirits of God sent forth into all the earth.

The phrase "and I beheld" means that John started looking for the Lion of Judah and the phrase "in the midst of the throne and of the four beasts" he didn't have to look far because Jesus stood and He looked like a Lamb; He was standing as a Lamb. The Lamb is standing in the midst of the throne preparing to present himself as a kinsman redeemer and he saw that "the Lamb had been slain", the Lamb had been violently murdered, because Jesus was wearing the marks of the crucifixion in His body for all eternity. "He had seven horns"; the word horn in the Old Testament symbolizes power and the number seven refers to complete. Jesus is the Lamb with complete power, He is omnipotent. "Has seven eyes" He has perception and He knows all. Again "seven Spirits of God sent forth into all the earth" refers to the Holy Spirit as being sent to the earth.

VERSE 7
And he came and took the book out of the right hand of him that sat upon the throne.

The Lamb "took the Book from the right hand of God" without hesitation, because Jesus is worthy! The Greek language literally reads that the Lamb has taken the Book from the right hand of God without hesitation because Jesus is worthy. Jesus takes the title deed to the earth which has been forfeited by sin. He claims our lost inheritance in Him. The one that sat upon the throne is a reference to God the Father.

VERSE 8
And when he had taken the book, the four beasts and four <and> twenty elders fell down before the Lamb, having

every one of them harps, and golden vials full of odors, which are the prayers of saints.

The phrase "four beasts" is literally four creatures. They are angelic beings before the throne of God. The twenty-four elders represent all the redeemed of the ages. A good cross reference for this would be Revelation 4:4. When Jesus, who is the lamb took the Book; all of the angels along with the redeemed of God fall before Him and worship Him.

The Bible says the elders had harps. This means they had in their hands instruments of Praise and golden bowls of incense. This is a picture of the prayers of the Saints.

New Song

VERSE 9

And they sung a new song, saying, Thou art worthy to take the book, and to open the seals thereof: for thou wast slain, and hast redeemed us to God by thy blood out of every kindred, and tongue, and people, and nation;

The Bible says that "they sung a new song". There are two Greek words for new. The word "NEOS" means now in time and the word "KAINOS" means new in character or kind. The word used to describe the song the elders sang is

"KAINOS" which means a new kind of song. Beloved there is never been a song like this song. New songs of praise are needed to express gratitude for new acts of God's mercy, but when the Lamb reclaims everything that already belongs to God there is a need for a new song and a new praise.

The Holy Spirit gives us a glimpse into the sound of this new song. He acknowledges that Jesus the Lamb is the rightful heir, He acknowledges that Jesus the Lamb was violently murdered meaning He was slain and in the process of our redemption was the crucifixion of the Lamb of God. He acknowledges that we have been redeemed by the blood of the Lamb. In other words, we have been bought by God. The Lamb of God was slain in order to purchase our salvation. Christ redemption is for all people. The Bible says, "Whosoever will let him come".

VERSE 10

And hast made us unto our God kings and priests: and we shall reign on the earth.

The phrase literally means a kingdom of priest. Because of the redemptive act of Jesus, we have become a kingdom unto God. We have become priests unto God.

The priests alone have the right to approach God and we have the right today to approach God simply because this is the price that Jesus has paid for us.

Also in this verse there is a reference to the millennium kingdom when we will reign with Christ on the earth for one thousand years.

VERSE 11
And I beheld, and I heard the voice of many angels round about the throne and the beasts and the elders: and the number of them was ten thousand times ten thousand, and thousands of thousands;

The word "many" in this passage of scripture means, "MYRIADS" of myriads and thousands of thousands, this phrase simply means, an innumerable host. All of heaven's host join in to praise the Lamb.

VERSE 12
Saying with a loud voice, Worthy is the Lamb that was slain to receive power, and riches, and wisdom, and strength, and honour, and glory, and blessing.

After the singing of the new song heaven's host cry out with a loud voice, a seven fold acclamation of the Lamb. It is written for our admonition here in verse 12... Power, Riches, Wisdom, Strength, Honour, Glory, and Blessing.

True Worship

VERSE 13

And every creature which is in heaven, and on the earth, and under the earth, and such as are in the sea, and all that are in them, I heard saying, Blessing, and honour, and glory, and power, <be> unto him that sitteth upon the throne, and unto the Lamb for ever and ever.

The four living creatures and the twenty-four elders are the first ones to praise God. Then of course the angels join in and every created thing joins in the heavenly host praising the Lamb which is Jesus. There is a repeat of this praise as if the verse is repeated in a new song, "Blessing, and honour, and glory and power" and of course this is a reference to the triune God who sits upon the throne and unto the Lamb which is Jesus in the midst of the throne. The phrase, "forever and ever" literally means unto the age of ages. The Greek language states that God is to be praised eternally because He is an eternal God. He is the one who created time and spoke it into existence.

VERSE 14

And the four beasts said, Amen. And the four <and> twenty elders fell down and worshipped him that liveth for ever and ever.

The grand chorus of praise is brought to a dramatic conclusion when the four angelic creatures come to say the word AMEN. The word AMEN simply means "so let it be".

REVELATION 6

VERSE BY VERSE

VERSE 1

And I saw when the Lamb opened one of the seals, and I heard, as it were the noise of thunder, one of the four beasts saying, Come and see.

When the Lamb has received the book He' begins the process of breaking the seals that have kept the secrets of God throughout the ages. As the seals are broken the events will occur between the Rapture of the church and the Return of our Lord to reign during His Millennium Kingdom, The use of the word "Thunder", is symbolic of an approaching storm. It is a picture of God's power and His judgment. In the first verse, when the seal is broken one of the four angelic creatures before the throne of God speaks. He says; "Come and see what God is about to do"

White Horse

VERSE 2

And I saw, and behold a white horse: and he that sat on him had a bow; and a crown was given unto him: and he in scripture went forth conquering, and to conquer.

This description is probably taken from Zachariah 1:8. In the Old Testament days the horse was an animal of war. The white horse was the horse ridden by the King and the victory processional after the war had been won. When we see the rider in the first seal that is on the white horse, it's symbolic of pace but this is not a picture of Jesus this is a picture of the Anti-Christ. The reason it is symbolic of peace is the fact that he had in his hand a bow which is a sign of military power in the Old Testament but he has no arrow. So when the Anti-Christ first comes on the scene he will come as a man of peace and he will deceive many. The Bible says a crown is given to him. The Anti-Christ will be empowered by Satan to try to conquer the world and he will go forth to reclaim Satan's domain.

VERSE 3
And when he had opened the second seal, I heard the second beast say, Come and see.

This is a picture of the second seal, and when the second seal opens we see that God's plan continues to proceed.

Red Horse

VERSE 4

And there went out another horse <that was> red: and <power> was given to him that sat thereon to take peace from the earth, and that they should kill one another: and there was given unto him a great sword.

This is a rider on a red horse and of course the red horse represents massive bloodshed. Power was given to him from Satan and this is a picture of the reign of the Anti-Christ when peace will be totally absent from the planet and war will be rampant everywhere. The Bible says; "that they will kill one another, it means to slaughter violently". The tribulation period will be characterized by war, violence and bloodshed.

Black Horse

VERSE 5

And when he had opened the third seal, I heard the third beast say, Come and see. And I beheld, and lo a black horse; and he that sat on him had a pair of balances in his hand.

This is a picture of the third seal and 1.1: is a picture of a black horse. The color black symbolizes mourning and famine. After war across the land when many of the young men have gone to war, the crops will have no one to tend them and there will be great famine.

VERSE 6
And I heard a voice in the midst of the four beasts say, A measure of wheat for a penny, and three measures of barley for a penny; and <see> thou hurt not the oil and the wine.,

This is a description of what the economic situation will be during the time when this seal is broken. The word measure in this passage of scripture is equivalent to about two pints. The wages in Jesus day was about a penny a day, the tribulation period will be characterized by tremendous inflation. Man will have to work all day to earn enough money to buy food himself not counting his family.

VERSE 7
And when he had opened the fourth seal, I heard the voice of the fourth beast say, Come and see.

This is a picture of the fourth seal which is about to be open and God's plan will continue to proceed.

Pale Horse

VERSE 8

And I looked, and behold a pale horse: and was Death, and Hell followed with him. And power was given unto them over the fourth part of the earth, to kill with sword, and with hunger, and with death, and with the beasts of the earth.

This is a picture of the rider on a pale horse which means a picture of death. It is also the same word used in the Hebrew language to describe one who has been stricken with some type of disease resulting in death. In this passage of scripture the rider is actually named, his name is Death and someone follows him and that is Hell. Of course the word Hell here refers to the abode of the dead beyond death. It seems that all power is given to this rider to inflict death upon thousands of people during the Tribulation period.

Altar of Sacrifice

VERSE 9

And when he had opened the fifth seal, I saw under the altar the souls of them that were slain for the Word of God, and for the testimony which they held:

Verse nine is a picture of the "opening of the fifth seal and John sees an altar" in Heaven. This is an altar of sacrifice, the souls of them that were slain for the Word of God. It is a picture of the multitude which no man can number. There will be many people during the tribulation period who will find Christ only to lose their physical life immediately upon receiving Christ as their personal Lord and Savior. The Bible says that they will be murdered because of their testimony.

VERSE 10

And they cried with a loud voice, saying How long, 0 Lord, holy and true, dost thou not judge and avenge our blood on them that dwell on the earth?

Verse ten is a picture of the Saints, they begin to cry out, as all the Saints of the ages are asking "How long 0 Lord"? How long before God puts Satan on the chain gang and places him in Hell forever and ever?

VERSE 11

And white robes were given unto every one of them; and it was said unto them, that they should rest yet for a little season, until their fellow servants also and their brethren, that should be killed as they <were>, should be fulfilled.

Universal Judgment

VERSE 12

And I beheld when he had opened the sixth seal, and, lo, there was a great earthquake; and the sun became black as sackcloth of hair, and the moon became as blood,

Verse twelve is a picture of the sixth seal and when it is opened by the Lamb we see a picture of God's universal judgment of all creation. The Bible says that the sun becomes black as sackcloth of hair, that means that the sun will be as black as goats hair and the moon will become as blood, the moon will have the appearance of blood and turn red in accordance to the Word of God, the whole earth will have a tremendous shaking.

VERSE 13

And the stars of heaven fell unto the earth, even as a fig tree cast her untimely figs, when she is shaken of a mighty wind.

The Bible says; that stars of heaven will fall to the earth and this is a picture of utter chaos and the fact that when the stars of Heaven fall there is no hope for those on earth.

VERSE 14

And the heaven departed as a scroll when it is rolled together; and every mountain and island were moved out of their places.

This is a picture of "a scroll being rolled out", held open and then this is released and allowed to suddenly roll together and this is another symbolic picture of chaos in the Heavens. Mountains will disappear and islands be removed from their places.

VERSE 15

And the kings of the earth, and the great men, and the rich men, and the chief captains, and the mighty men, and every bondman, and every free man, hid themselves in the dens and in the rocks of the mountains;

The reigning monarchs of this earth will all be a part of this human tragedy. No one will escape the judgment of God. Governors, princes, presidents, people who have wealth, people who are commanders, people who are mighty, people who are slaves, people who are free to go wherever they want; will cry for the rocks and mountains to fall on them. They will hide in caves. Social status among the human race and society will mean nothing in these days.

VERSE 16

And said to the mountains and rocks, Fall on us, and hide us from the face of him that sits on the throne, and from the wrath of the Lamb;

The Bible says "they will cry for the rocks to fall upon them, they will try to hide from the face of God", from the presence of God. Man has been trying to do that since the first Adam fell.

VERSE 17

For the great day of his wrath is come; and who shall be able to stand?

The word "day" here means a specified period of time not necessarily a twenty-four hour period. The Tribulation period will be the time when God's wrath is poured out on the earth in full strength and no one will be able to stand.

REVELATION 7

VERSE 1

And after these things I saw four angels standing on the four corners of the earth, holding the four winds of the earth, that the wind should not blow on the earth, nor on the sea, nor on any tree.

There is an interlude between the breaking of the sixth and seventh seals of the book. The first, six seals have been given us a description of the terrible judgment that God is going to pour out on the earth. But in the seventh seal we are going to see a great revival that the world has never witnessed before or during the Tribulation period. When you get to this passage of scripture, many people who have built denominations on this text. But the Bible says that after the breaking of the six seals that John saw the four angels. Of course four is symbolic number of the earth and they were standing on four corners of the earth refer to the whole world. And they were holding the four winds of the earth which describe the terrible storm that is coming during the Tribulation.

VERSE 2

And I saw another angel ascending from the east, having the seal of the living God: and he cried with a loud voice to the four angels, to whom it was given to hurt the earth and the sea,

The concept of the seal of God is very familiar during Bible days. The King wore a ring which contained a seal. This seal implied its possession and protection. The one hundred and forty-four thousand that are sealed during this time, is a picture of the one hundred and forty-four thousand converted Jews who become God's great ministers to carry the gospel through this period of the Tribulation.

VERSE 3

Saying, Hurt not the earth, neither the sea, nor the trees, till we have sealed the servants of our God in their foreheads.

This halt in judgment is only temporary, it is going to resume very soon. The servants of God have been sealed and this is the picture of those who believe now that Jesus is the Messiah and that and Anti-Christ is Satan. They preach to the world that Jesus is the Messiah that He is the Son of God and He is the only one who can bring true Salvation.

144,000 Witnesses

VERSE 4

And I heard the number of them which were sealed: <and there were> sealed an hundred <and> forty <and> four thousand of all the tribes of the children of Israel.

This is the text I was referencing to concerning the many denominations that have spun from this passage of scripture. Jehovah Witnessess, Seventh Day Advent Groups, The Mormon Elders, Herbert W. Armstrong Group, they all believe this one hundred and forty-four thousand represent the Universal Church, but that is not what the Bible teaches. These are sealed Jews who are saved during the Tribulation period and as I said before the message of the fact that Jesus is the Messiah will be a message which will be carried not only to the nation Israel but all over the world.

VERSE 5

Of the tribe of Judah <were> sealed twelve thousand. Of the tribe of Reuben <were> sealed twelve thousand. Of the tribe of Gad <were> sealed twelve thousand.

Here we see twelve thousand from each of the tribes of Judah are to be sealed.

VERSE 6

Of the tribe of Aser <were> sealed twelve thousand. Of the tribe of Nephthalim <were> sealed twelve thousand. Of the tribe of Manasses <were> sealed twelve thousand.

Verse six is a continuation of the listing of these tribes

VERSE 7

Of the tribe of Simeon <were> sealed twelve thousand. Of the tribe of Levi <were> sealed twelve thousand. Of the tribe of Issachar <were> sealed twelve thousand.

Verse seven is a continuation of the listing of these tribes.

VERSE 8

Of the tribe of Zabulon <were> sealed twelve thousand. Of the tribe of Joseph <were> sealed twelve thousand. Of the tribe of Benjamin <were> sealed twelve thousand.

Verse eight is a continuation of the listing of these tribes.

VERSE 9

After this I beheld, and, lo, a great multitude, which no man could number, of all nations, and kindreds and people, and tongues, stood before the throne, and before the Lamb, clothed with white robes, and palms in their hands;

This signifies the end of the sealing of the one hundred and forty-four thousand Jews. The Bible says, that after the rapture of the church that there will only be non-believers left on the earth and many of them will be defiant against God and will not repent. But once the one hundred and forty-four thousand Jews have been sealed and they preach the gospel many people will come to know Jesus Christ as their personal Lord and Savior. The Bible says, all nations and kindreds and people and tongues will stand before the Lamb. They will be clothed with white robes, they will have palms in their hands.

VERSE 10

And cried with a loud voice, saying, Salvation to our God which sitteth upon the throne, and unto the Lamb.

The phrase literally means, Salvation is from our God. It means that God accomplished Salvation and delivered us through the act of the Lamb has taken on the Cross.

VERSE 11

And all the angels stood round about the throne, and <about> the elders and the four beasts, and fell before the throne on their faces, and worshipped God,

As we have already seen, the elders represent all the redeemed of God. The four beast literally means the four living creatures and they fall into worship before God.

VERSE 12
Saying, Amen: Blessing, and glory, and wisdom, and thanksgiving, and honour, and power, and might, <be> unto our God for ever and ever. Amen.

This is a praise song of Thanksgiving that is laid at the feet of God for He alone is worthy.

VERSE 13
And one of the elders answered, saying unto me, What are these which are arrayed in white robes? and whence came they?

John asked the question, "who are these people and where did they come from?"

VERSE 14
And I said unto him, Sir, thou knowest. And he said to me, These are they which came out of great tribulation, and have washed their robes, and made them white in the blood of the Lamb.

This is a confession of ignorance by the apostle John and he knows that God knows who they are. The verb "have come" is a present middle participle, it conveys the idea of continued repetition. It means these are the ones who are continually coming out of great Tribulation. So there will be a great multitude of people who will be saved because there robes will have been washed white by the blood of the Lamb.

VERSE 15

Therefore are they before the throne of God, and serve him day and night in his temple: and he that sitteth on the throne shall dwell among them.

These martyred Tribulation Saints have been persecuted under our God and will spend eternity serving Him. This verse deals with their service to Him.

VERSE 16

They shall hunger no more, neither thirst any more: neither shall the sun light on them, nor any heat.

They will not have to go through the Tribulation period: that has been characterized by famine and war and death. They will not have to worry anymore concerning heat and light which is a characteristic of the great Tribulation period. Great heat, the turning of the moon black, a third of the sun, moon and stars being blackened later in the other judgments are listed in the Book of the Revelation concerning the Tribulation period.

VERSE 17

For the Lamb which is in the midst of the throne shall feed them, and shall lead them unto living fountains of waters: and God shall wipe away all tears from their eyes.

This is a picture of Jesus that is seated in the middle of the throne and it means that He is a gentle Shepherd and He is going to be the Shepherd of all these that have washed in the blood of the Lamb. He is our Faithful Guide. As a result of Jesus nourishment to the spiritual body of the church; the Bible says, here that God will wipe away all tears from their eyes. So the song entitled "No Tears in Heaven" is not theologically correct. There will be tears in heaven because the Bible says that God will wipe away all tears.

REVELATION 8

VERSE BY VERSE

VERSE 1

And when he had opened the seventh seal, there was silence in heaven about the space of half an hour.

This is a picture of when the seventh seal is opened and there is literally-"silence". There was silent when He created the heavens and the earth and He rested in the seventh day. The Bible says, this is about the space of half an hour , it refers to a brief period of time, but all of earth and heaven will be silent, especially heaven.

VERSE 2

And I saw the seven angels which stood before God; and to them were given seven trumpets.

The seven angels here are archangels this means they are the first ones to stand in the presence of God and they enjoyed a special place of privilege and honor. They are about to blow seven trumpets that will get the attention of the people not only in Heaven but on the earth below.

Prayers of Saints

VERSE 3

And another angel came and stood at the altar, having a golden censer; and there was given unto him much incense, that he should offer <it> with the prayers of all saints upon the golden altar which was before the throne.

This angel is not one of the seven angels in the presence of God. This angel has stood before the altar of incense and this is a sacrificial altar which was seen in the Old Testament and also a picture of Revelation 6:9. He holds in His hand a golden censer and he takes the hot coals from the altar. This incense offered unto God is a picture of the prayers of His people.

VERSE 4

And the smoke of the incense, <which came> with the prayers of the saints, ascended up before God out of the angel's hand.

All the prayers of all the Saints will one day come before the throne of God and the martyred Saints are crying out to God "Lord, how long, how long"?

VERSE 5

And the angel took the censer, and filled it with fire of the altar, and cast <it> into the earth: and there were voices, and thunderings, and lightnings, and an earthquake.

The angel takes the censer and fills it with fire off the altar, and he cast it upon the earth in fiery judgment. It is a picture of an approaching storm with the blowing of the first trumpet.

VERSE 6

And the seven angels which had the seven trumpets prepared themselves to sound.

The seven angels prepare themselves they practices blowing the trumpets and getting ready.

VERSE 7

The first angel sounded, and there followed hail and fire mingled with blood, and they were cast upon the earth: and the third part of trees was burnt up, and all green grass was burnt up.

The first trumpet is blown and down upon the earth falls Hell and fire mingled with blood. This is a picture of the plague that fell upon Egypt in Exodus 9. This is going to destroy the vegetation on the earth and cause great famine. A third of the trees will be burnt and all of the green grass will be burnt.

VERSE 8

And the second angel sounded, and as it were a great mountain burning with fire was cast into the sea: and the third part of the sea became blood;

This picture of the second trumpet that has sounded and once again this is a judgment that is similar to the first Egyptian plague. It is possible that this might be a volcano. During this time a third part of the sea turns into blood and a mountain burning with fire is cast into the sea. Can you imagine what happens when the third part of the sea turns to blood and all the fish in that portion of the sea die and float to the top? Ships will no longer be able to sail.

VERSE 9

And the third part of the creatures which were in the sea, and had life, died; and the third part of the ships were destroyed.

A third part of the creatures which were in the sea have died and float to the top as I said this is a judgment that is similar to the black horse that we have already talked about which cause great famine.

The ships will not be able to sail the seas, this will have a profound economic effect on the international market.

VERSE 10
And the third angel sounded, and there fell a great star from heaven, burning as it were a lamp, and it fell upon the third part of the rivers, and upon the fountains of waters;

With the sounding of the third trumpet, a star from heaven that is on fire like a lamp will fall. Meteorites fall to the earth this is again what is seen in Exodus 9 and this judgment is upon fresh water making it undrinkable. A third of the rivers and fountains and springs will make the water undrinkable, and so we see not only the salt water has been smitten but a third of all the fresh water and streams have been smitten

VERSE 11
And the name of the star is called Wormwood: and the third part of the waters became wormwood; and many men died of the waters, because they were made bitter.

This star is named that fell from heaven, it is called Wormwood. It's named after a plant that is in the Old Testament; and it means "bitter sorrow".

VERSE 12

And the fourth angel sounded, and the third part of the sun was smitten, and the third part of the moon, and the third part of the stars; so as the third part of them was darkened, and the day shone not for a third part of it, and the night likewise.

When the fourth trumpet sounds a third part of the sun is smitten and a third part of the moon. This corresponds with the ninth Egyptian plague in Exodus 10. The hours of light will be reduced on earth to one third.

VERSE 13

And I beheld, and heard an angel flying through the midst of heaven, saying with a loud voice, Woe, woe, woe, to the inhibitors of the earth by reason of the other voices of the trumpet of the three angels, which are yet to sound!

This is a picture of an angel, (in the Greek language translated an Eagle) which is a picture of a symbol of majesty and power. It cries with a loud voice so that everyone can hear that the worst is yet to come.

REVELATION 9

VERSE 1

And the fifth angel sounded, and I saw a star fall from heaven unto the earth: and to him was given the key of the bottomless pit.

This is the fifth trumpet that is sounded and a star falls from heaven to the earth the word in the Greek here literally means "heaven fallen". Satan was given the key to the bottomless pit, the word pit is "the abyss". It refers to a prison house in which millions of fallen angels and demons are imprisoned after Satan was cast out of heaven. God will give Satan the key to the bottomless pit and allow him to free these demons that have been held captive since their rebellion in heaven and eternity past.

Smoke of Pit

VERSE 2

And he opened the bottomless pit; and there arose a smoke out of the pit, as the smoke of a great furnace; and the sun and the air were darkened by reason of the smoke of the pit.

The Bible says smoke will come up out of the pit like a great furnace symbolizing violence, corruption, destruction, attributed by these demonic beings. The sun in the air will be darkened from this smoke of this pit.

VERSE 3

And there came out of the smoke locusts upon the earth: and unto them was given power, as the scorpions of the earth have power.

Out of the billowing smoke will be hoards of demon spirits that John refers to as locust. This are not insects, they are used to describe demon spirits because of their destructive nature. The locusts in Bible days were one of the most dreaded insects in the lands of Israel and Judah. The tail of the scorpion contains a gland that secrets poisonous fluid, and these demonic beings have the power to inflict great pain with their tails.

VERSE 4

And it was commanded them that they should not hurt the grass of the earth, neither any green things, neither any tree; but only those men which have not the seal of God in their foreheads.

This reminds us that they are not ordinary locust because they are not going to devour any vegetation. All of the people that did not receive the seal of God are afflicted by these demon locust.

VERSE 5

And to them it was given that they should not kill them, but that they should be tormented five months: and their torment <was> as the torment of a scorpion, when he strikes a man.

The demon locusts are under the command of a superior and they do not kill mankind they just torment them. The Bible says for five months. This just lets us know that God is limiting the time of their destructive power. There is a reference to the scorpion.

VERSE 6

And in those days shall men seek death, and shall not find it; and shall desire to die, and death shall flee from them.

The Bible says that things will be so bad that death will be an escape. Men will try to die and God will not permit it. Jeremiah spoke of that day when men would chose death rather than life.

Demon Locusts

VERSE 7

And the shapes of the locusts <were> like unto horses prepared unto battle; and on their heads <were> as it were crowns like gold, and their faces <were> as the faces of men.

This is the description of the shapes of these demon locust. The horse was the animal of war and John saw these demons as an army making war against humanity. They had crowns of gold and their faces were the faces of men, they had the intelligence of man.

VERSE 8

And they had hair as the hair of women, and their teeth were as <the teeth> of lions.

They had the hair as hair of women which is a picture of shrewdness, seductiveness.

VERSE 9

And they had breastplates as it were breastplates of iron; and the sound of their wings <was> as the sound of chariots of many horses running to battle.

The demon locust had breastplates of iron illustration their indestructibility. They make a tremendous sound as massive chariots roaring across the land.

VERSE 10

And they had tails like unto scorpions, and there were stings in their tails: and their power <was> to hurt men five months.

The tails had stings in it and they could have the ability to torment and afflict pain on mankind. The Bible says again that God wills this to happen and gives them a time frame.

VERSE 11

And they had a king over them, <which is> the angel of the bottomless pit, whose name in the Hebrew tongue <is> Abaddon, but in the Greek tongue hath <his> name Apollyon.

They have a commander and chief which is over them, he is the angel of the bottomless pit. The angel is a high ranking, fallen angel that Satan has selected. He is listed here in Hebrew and Greek "his word means destroyer".

VERSE 12

One woe is past; <and>, behold, there come two woes more hereafter.

The first "woe" with the fifth trumpet has past and two more remains.

VERSE 13
And the sixth angel sounded, and I heard a voice from the four horns of the golden altar which is before God,

This is the same altar from which the prayer of the saints have already ascended. This was the altar of incense and the horns on the altar always have been a picture of a place of mercy.

VERSE 14
Saying to the sixth angel which had the trumpet, Loose the four angels which are bound in the great river Euphrates.

These four angels are not holy angels but they are fallen angels. The Bible mentions certain groups of fallen angels. The Bible mentions certain groups of fallen angels that have been imprisoned. The river Euphrates is the ancient border between Israel and all of her enemies.

VERSE 15
And the four angels were loosed, which were prepared for an hour, and a day, and a month, and a year, for to slay the third part of men.

The angels who are evil are holding in their hands this terrible power of destruction until God has allowed them to destroy at this particular time in the Tribulation period and they kill a third part of all the men on the earth.

VERSE 16
And the number of the army of the horsemen <were> two hundred million: and I heard the number of them.

We know this massive demon driven army has two hundred million that are loosed by these four evil angels.

VERSE 17
And thus I saw the horses in the vision, and them that sat on them, having breastplates of fire, and of jacinth, and brimstones: and the heads of the horses <were> as the heads of lions; and out of their mouths issued fire and smoke and brimstone.

Here again is a description of these riders. They have smoked colored breastplates WHICH MEANS THE POWER TO CREATE FIRE, A PICTURE OF SULFUR AND BRIMSTONE. These are not ordinary horses they have heads of a lion which symbolizes their ferociousness. Out of their mouth they have the power to exhibit fire.

VERSE 18

By these three was the third part of men killed, by fire, and by the smoke, and by the brimstone, which issued out of their mouths.

Once again a third of all mankind, one fourth of the earth's population has already been killed prior to this and at this point over half the population of the earth has been destroyed.

VERSE 19

For their power is in their mouth, and in their tails: for their tails <were> like unto serpents, and had heads, and with them they do hurt.

The power is in their mouth and in their tails which proceeds from the horse's mouth and also from their tails and the serpent is a reference to Satan.

VERSE 20

And the rest of the men which were not killed by these plagues yet repented not of the works of their hands, that they should not worship devils, and idols of gold, and silver, and brass, and stone, and of wood: which neither can see, nor hear, nor walk:

The rest of the men that were not killed by these plague are those who survived the catastrophe of which has taken place on the earth such as war, and famine. Many of them have not repented and are still doing the same deeds that they did, the deeds of wickedness, the first deed listened as idolatry, and demon worship. They still do not worship the true living God.

VERSE 21

Neither repented they of their murders, nor of their sorceries, nor of their fornication, nor of their thefts.

They are still violent people that have little regard for human life. They use medicine, drugs, and spells they use drugs that are in drug trafficking, they have nothing for the sanctity of a marriage relationship. Holiness is not in their vocabulary. They have no regard for personal property.

REVELATION 10

VERSE BY VERSE

The first four trumpets show us humans as citizens of a sin-blighted world; everything above and around them tells of the curse brought by their fall.

The fifth trumpet presents humans as the actual sinners and shows us the whole world "lying in the wicked one." Humans sin and are therefore of the devil, and their sins bring hell-sent torments.

The sixth trumpet makes it clear that judgment come upon sinners by virtue of the fixed law that sin must inevitably bring suffering. The divinely inflicted judgments remind us that God is angry with the wicked every day.

In between the 6th and 7th trumpet

1. Mighty Angel

2. Bittersweet Book

3. Measuring Reed

4. Two Witnesses

THE MIGHTY ANGEL (10:1-7)

VERSE 1
I saw still another mighty angel coming down from heaven, clothed with a cloud. And a rainbow was on his head, his face was like the sun, and his feet like pillars of fire.

VERSE 2
He had a little book open in his hand. And he set his right foot on the sea and his left foot on the land

VERSE 3
and cried with a loud voice, as when a lion roars. When he cried out, seven thunders uttered their voices.

VERSE 4
Now when the seven thunders uttered their voices, I was about to write; but I heard a voice from heaven saying to me, "Seal up the things which the seven thunders uttered, and do not write them."

VERSE 5
The angel whom I saw standing on the sea and on the land raised up his hand to heaven

VERSE 6
and swore by Him who lives forever and ever, who created heaven and the things that are in it, the earth and the things

that are in it, and the sea and the things that are in it, that there should be delay no longer

VERSE 7

but in the days of the sounding of the seventh angel, when he is about to sound, the mystery of God would be finished, as He declared to His servants the prophets.

Between the sixth and seventh trumpets we have an impressive and significant parenthesis, containing one of the most profound yet simple sections of Revelation. In it, John sees the mighty angel, the little book, the measuring rod, the two witnesses, and the earthquake.

Things are now drawing to a close. The first half on Daniel's seventieth week is nearly spent; its last days show the world in open rebellion against God and His people, upon whom the beast and the antichrist pour out their fury. But before the last dregs of the Lord's vengeance are drunk by the Gentile and Jewish apostates and their followers, this consoling vision breaks through the dark clouds of judgement. It is a stern reminder to the world that, in spite of the raging of the wicked, the government of the earth is the just claim of the Creator- a claim that will now be made good in power. The vision is also designed to strengthen and console believers, and especially suffering believers, for the same power that will crush the enemy will exalt the sufferers to honor.

THE MIGHTY ANGEL (10:1-7)

Then the angel I had seen standing on the sea...said, "There will be no more delay." (Revelation 10:6)

Who is this glorious angel who occupies heaven, earth, and the sea? God's chariot is in the clouds (Psalm 104:4) and sends forth this angel who comes with glory. Some versions speak of him as a "strong angel." Some writers see in him the herald angel announcing the solemn crisis under the third woe or seventh trumpet (11:15-19). Because the word "angel" does not necessarily mean an individual member of the angelic race, but often denotes a thing or person in active service, can it be that this "mighty angel" is Christ Himself, coming forth to act on behalf of His faithful people? Let us look at the separate features of this awesome being who dominates the universe.

Christ not only leaves heaven as a place of departure, He also comes "down from heaven" as His native home (10:1). Providential dealings with earth are about to cease, so the

Lord leaves His abode to establish His worldwide kingdom once His judgment work is finished. How the angelic and redeemed hosts in heaven will praise Him as he leaves their presence to take to Himself His power to reign!

Christ is "robed in a cloud" (10:1). The rainbow that surrounded the throne (4:3) now encircles the head of the mighty angel. The rainbow symbolizes the fact of a kept covenant, and by it God's faithful remnant is assured that even amidst the fiercest conflict they are secure and need feel no fear. Christ is coming as the Messenger of the covenant-keeping God, and He will call the earth to witness that. But He is about to break His covenant because the world has rejected it. What a glorious sight He will present with His head diademed with a magnificent rainbow!

Christ's face is as the sun, and His feet are as fire (10:1). Here we have a repetition of what we saw in the Patmos vision (1:15-16). The double metaphor of sun and fire speaks of the supreme, searching, and fixed character of the message about to be given. Taken together, the sun-like face and feet as pillars of fire can suggest Christ's supreme majesty and His eternal stability as earth experiences the unbending holiness of His judicial mission.

Christ has a little book in His hand (10:2). The word for "book" comes from biblos, from which we get Bible. Here is a "little bible," a larger version of which is the seven-sealed book of chapter 5. The "little" book is open, but the larger book was sealed, then opened by the Lamb. It is open for all who read its unmistakable message.

Christ's right foot is on the sea, and His left foot is on the earth (10:2). In this bold and graphic picture, the mighty Angel is presented as a colossal figure standing astride both land and sea. As the Lord of creation, He dominates the scene entirely.

It has been asked whether there is any special significance in the position of the feet. There certainly is! The sea-turbulent, agitated and restless- represents the chaotic, revolutionary condition of the nations. The earth, which humans have partially harnessed, symbolizes the orderly government of civilized and educated people. Three times over the angel is depicted as standing on sea and earth (10:2,5,8), and this repetition denotes divine emphasis. The strong and sure tread of Christ's feet of fine brass signifies the complete subjugation of all people and forces in the world to Him.

Human and natural forces everywhere will acknowledge His dominion as He exercised both His right and His might.

Christ's voice is like a lion's roar (10:3). Here we have another feature of "the voice of many waters." No voice is more feared by people and beats in the jungle than the roar of the lion. Loud, roaring voices are not always intelligible, but there will be no mistaking the meaning of the roar of the Lion of Judah as it causes intense terror and despair (Psalm 68:33; Hosea 11:10; Joel 3:16). In the wonderful voice psalm (Psalm 29) we are given a sevenfold description of the Lord's majestic voice.

If the lion's roar suggests irresistible power, the seven thunders (10:3) speak of the terror of the Lord in all its completeness as He comes in judgment. Just what the nature of this judgment is we are not told, as John was commanded not to write what the thunders said (10:4) Ten times over thunder occurs in Revelation, and because the thundering's proceed out of the throne they have a divine message and mission. Job speaks of "the thunder of His power" (Job 26:14), and while Jesus was here on earth the voice of God seemed like thunder to some who heard it (John 12:28-29).

Thunder is God's voice in judgment, the expression of His authority therein.

Like Daniel's visions, the contents of the seven thunders had to be closed and sealed. John understood them and knew that they were the perfection of God's intervention in judgment, but the divine command as to their nature was, "Do not write it down." Much of the prophetic section of revelation will be fully understood only as the predicated actually take place.

When Jesus ascended to heaven, He lifted up His hands in priestly benediction of His own people. Now, as He descends, His hand is lifted up to heaven (10:5) as if through an oath He will fulfill the righteous judgment of God's holy throne. A hand lifted up to heaven was a customary gesture in taking an oath (Genesis 14:22; Deuteronomy 32:40; Daniel 12:7). We have here one of the most sublime visions in Revelation. Try to visualize the scene: the mighty Angel of Jehovah, with the sea and earth under His feet; the book of closing prophecy in His left hand, and His right hand lifted up to heaven, swearing by the ever living God and Creator that judgment upon the godless will be immediate.

How are we to understand the phrase "there will be no more delay" or "time no longer?" Can it be that the age-old cry for retribution, "How long, O Lord?" (Psalm 13:1-2; Revelation 6:10) is about to be answered, and humanity's day will now end in sharp and severe judgment? As we have seen, "seven" suggests perfection, and the seven trumpets and seven thunders signify the perfect completeness for God's warning judgment. No space is left for anything else to transpire before the final judgment, of which all previous judgments have been previous. In virtue of His native right and His redemptive work, Christ returns to consummate the judgment committed to Him by the Father (John 5:22, 27).

The world "revelation" implies an unveiling of a mystery; here, the mystery of God (10:7) that was foretold by the prophets and apostles is about to be finished (Romans 16:25-26; Ephesians 1:9-10, etc.). Now we see so many things in a glass darkly- for example, the mystery of God's apparent silence when His saints are crushed and cruelly persecuted. As a God of justice, why does He allow terrible sins to go unpunished, and why does He not intervene to right the wrongs of the earth?

The mystery John speaks about may be the brutal martyrdom of the Tribulation saints and the silence of heaven about this terrible wrong. But the mystery is about to end. Christ appears to wrest world government from the grasp of Satan, to expel him as the usurper, and to end his tyranny on earth. The mystery of divine patience for over six millennia is now about to cease. The judgment hour has come for God to fully and finally avenge His own elect who have cried out to Him day and night.

How moving is Hervey's eloquent tribute to John's unrivaled description of the "mighty Angel" (from Hervey's Meditations):

Observe the aspect of this august Personage. All the brightness of the sun shines in His countenance, and all the rage of fire burns in His feet. See His apparel! The clouds compose His robe, and the drapery of the sky floats upon His shoulders; the rainbow forms His diadem, and that which compasses heaven with a glorious circle is the ornament of His head. Behold His attitude! One foot stands on the ocean, and other rests on the land. The wide extended earth and the world of waters serve as pedestals of those mighty columns. Consider His action! His hand is lifted up to the height of the stars; he speaks, and the regions of the firmament echo with the mighty accents as the midnight desert resounds with the lion's roar. The artillery of the skies is discharged as a signal; a peal of sevenfold thunder spreads the alarm and prepares the universe to receive His orders. To finish all, and give the highest grandeur, as well as the utmost solemnity, to the representation, He swears by Him who lives forever and ever.

THE BITTERSWEET BOOK (10:8-11)

VERSE 8
Then the voice which I heard from heaven spoke to me again and said, "Go, take the little book which is open in the hand of the angel who stands on the sea and on the earth."

VERSE 9
So I went to the angel and said to him, "Give me the little book." And he said to me, "Take and eat it; and it will make your stomach bitter, but it will be as sweet as honey in your mouth."

VERSE 10
Then I took the little book out of the angel's hand and ate it, and it was as sweet as honey in my mouth. But when I had eaten it, my stomach became bitter.

VERSE 11
And he said to me, "You must prophesy again about many people, nations, tongues, and kings."

It tasted sweet as honey in my mouth, but when I had eaten it, my stomach turned sour. (Revelation 10:10)

John is now commanded to take and eat the little book that he saw in the hand of the mighty Angel. We can safely assume that the contents of this volume were the counsels and prophecies of the rest of Scripture, from Genesis to Jude. The time has now come to declare the divine counsel to peoples, nations, tongues, and rules. John must mentally digest the message of the book and then declare it.

Several times in Scripture, God's Word is compared to food that must be assimilated. Ezekiel, like John, experienced the sweet taste of prophecy (Ezekiel 2:8; 3:1-3). Jeremiah likewise had to consume the divine word (Jeremiah 15:16). The first effect of the prophetic communication was an unbounded delight as John saw how past predictions were about to be fulfilled. It was sweet to his taste to realize that at last earth's rule was to pass from Satan to Christ, and an evil age was about to end and a new era begin.

But then the apostle meditated on the effects of judgment upon the multitudes without God, and he thought of the final wrath under the seven vials and the terrors if the Lord about to overtake the godless. As he pondered the final doom of the lost, anguish gripped John's heart.

What was sweet to his taste would have a bitter effect upon rebellious earth dwellers. His commission was renewed, and out John had to go, prophesying to the multitudes about judgment to come.

For all preachers in this age of grace, the same principle holds. They must receive a God-given message and absorb it into their own being. Secondhand, unexperienced truth is never dynamic. Both the sweetness and the bitterness of a God-revealed gospel must be part of the spiritual training of heralds. Truth that they delight to receive demands the death of the self-life and a taste of the bitterness that comes from the hardships and disappointments of true witness bearing.

REVELATION 11

VERSE BY VERSE

THE MEASURING REED (11:1-2)

VERSE 1

Then I was given a reed like a measuring rod. And the angel stood, saying, "Rise and measure the temple of God, the altar, and those who worship there.

VERSE 2

"But leave out the court which is outside the temple, and do not measure it, for it has been given to the Gentiles. And they will tread the holy city underfoot for forty-two months.

The reed, a measuring instrument about ten feet in length, is frequently mentioned by the prophets of the Old Testament. Ezekiel speaks of the measuring rod being applied to the temple (Ezekiel 40:3; 42:16 20). In the New Jerusalem an angel measures the glorified church with a golden reed (21:15); here John uses a wooden reed to measure the temple. Such a measuring suggests the appropriation, preservation, and acceptance by God of temple, altar, and worshiper.

Mention of the court and the temple reveals that we are approaching Jewish ground. In fact, the whole chapter is anticipative. The Jews are to be back in their own land, and the temple is to be rebuilt. As a whole, the trumpets section deals with the devastation of Gentile, Christianized lands and peoples, but now judgment is about to be transferred from the Gentile to the Jew.

God's dealings with the apostate part of the Gentile world are about to conclude. The times of the Gentiles have run their course. We now approach the second half of Daniel's seventieth week, which is the last half of the Tribulation era. The man of sin makes a covenant with the Jews for seven years, but turns traitor halfway through the period. The agony of Israel's closing hour of unbelief during this time is here depicted.

This period covering the trampling of the Gentiles is given in different forms. Forty-two months, each thirty days long, correspond to the 1,260 days of the two witnesses. These forty-two months, or 1,260 days, make three and one-half years, which are equivalent to a "time" (one year), "times" (two years), and "half time" (one-half year), as stated in Daniel 12:7 (see also Revelation 11:3; 12:6, 14; 1:5).

This period is the duration of the blasphemy and power of the beast. Such a denomination of time is also referred to as "the midst of the week" (Daniel 9:27). Jerusalem's coming agony, then, is limited to forty- two months. And this will be long enough as she drinks the cup of the Lord's fury.

THE TWO WITNESSES (11:3-14)

VERSE 3
"And I will give power to my two witnesses, and they will prophesy one thousand two hundred and sixty days, clothed in sackcloth."

VERSE 4
These are the two olive trees and the two lampstands standing before the God of the earth.

VERSE 5
And if anyone wants to harm them, fire proceeds from their mouth and devours their enemies. And if anyone wants to harm them, he must be killed in this manner.

VERSE 6
These have power to shut heaven, so that no rain falls in the days of their prophecy; and they have power over waters to turn them to blood, and to strike the earth with all plagues, as often as they desire.

VERSE 7

When they finish their testimony, the beast that ascends out of the bottomless pit will make war against them, overcome them, and kill them.

VERSE 8

And their dead bodies will lie in the street of the great city which spiritually is called Sodom and Egypt, where also our Lord was crucified.

VERSE 9

Then those from the peoples, tribes, tongues, and nations will see their dead bodies three-and-a-half days, and not allow their dead bodies to be put into graves.

VERSE 10

And those who dwell on the earth will rejoice over them, make merry, and send gifts to one another, because these two prophets tormented those who dwell on the earth.

VERSE 11

Now after the three-and-a-half days the breath of life from God entered them, and they stood on their feet, and great fear fell on those who saw them.

VERSE 12

And they heard a loud voice from heaven saying to them, "Come up here." And they ascended to heaven in a cloud, and their enemies saw them.

VERSE 13

In the same hour there was a great earthquake, and a tenth of the city fell. In the earthquake seven thousand people were killed, and the rest were afraid and gave glory to the God of heaven.

VERSE 14

The second woe is past. Behold the third woe is coming quickly.

As to the identity of the two witnesses, the language points to two well-known characters. The article is emphatic—"the two witness of men." Therefore they must have been known at least to John.

What else do we know about these two inspired witnesses who are to be raised up to minister encouragement to the afflicted? John does not give us any clue to their identity, but simply describes them as witnesses, olive trees, lampstands, and prophets. (One witness may be John himself. See 10:11.) "The two olive trees" takes us back to Joshua and

Zerubbabel (Zechariah 3-4), who ministered to the Jewish people, just as the two olive trees emptied the oil out of themselves into the bowl of the lampstand (Zechariah 4:11-14). The "two witnesses" in the Tribulation period are to be channels of the oil feeding the remnant, and symbols of coming peace. The Holy Spirit will be the oil in them, making their ministry of encouragement possible.

As "lampstands," these witnesses are to give a sure and clear testimony. Their ministry will be exercised in the clear light of God because they stand before the Lord of the earth. As representative light bearers, they will testify that the One who was so widely disowned on earth is now about to be recognized openly as the rightful King over all. As "prophets" (11:10), they will preach in such a faithful way as to make people conscience stricken. Sin with its tragic consequences is a tormenting subject to even the most hardened and scarred conscience. Thus these witnesses are to have a tormenting ministry by the plagues they have power to inflict, and also by their testimony against their human environment.

The two witnesses are to prophesy clothed in sackcloth, that is, in a dress suited to their message. Sackcloth was the garment of prophets when they called the people to repentance. Their exterior appearance accorded with their words (Joel 1:13; I Kings 20:31). Perhaps sackcloth is a catchword, linking this episode under the sixth trumpet with the one under the sixth seal where "the sun turned black like sackcloth" (6:12) in righteous retribution on the apostates who rejected God's righteousness.

The days of their prophecy, or preaching, under the inspiration of the Spirit (a message of judgment against apostates) are to be 1,260. They are not to give an intermittent testimony. Daily they will testify until the allotted period is exhausted – a period that covers the last half of Daniel's week, or the great Tribulation proper.

Unlimited, delegated power is to be granted these witnesses. They will perform miracles "as often as they want" (11:6), repeating those that Moses and Elijah performed against slavery and apostasy: turning water into blood (Exodus 7:17) and withholding rain (I Kings 17:1).

But the two preachers in sackcloth are "immortal till their work is done." The immediate certainty of the accomplishment of their mission is indicated by the phrases "if anyone tries to harm them" (two times 11:5) and "they have finished their testimony" (11:7). Prophesying in Jerusalem, the center of the prophetic and political interest during the three and one-half years of the Tribulation, they are invincible until their dynamic and spectacular task is over.

The conclusion of the prophecy of the two witnesses is to be marked by a violent death. "The beast [or "the wild beast," as the original has it]...comes up from the Abyss." Nothing less than the antichrist, who is here mentioned for the first time in Revelation, will satisfy the picture here. The beast is fully described in Daniel 7:8, 11 and Revelation 13:1, a sure proof of the unity of Scripture. The triumph of this beast, who exceeds in cruelty and blasphemy any previous wickedness that has appeared upon the earth, is evidently complete, for the witnesses are silenced and slain. Martyrdom and massacres of the saints in all ages find their climax here. With the killing of divinely empowered witnesses, brute force appears to triumph over truth and righteousness.

To add to the humiliation and scornful treatment of the two witnesses, their bodies are allowed to remain in the street for the same number of days as the years of their ministry. For three and one-half days the spectators gloat over the dead bodies with a delight that is both fiendish and childish.

"Sodom and Egypt," as applied to Jerusalem (11:8), stand as a symbol of oppression and slavery. "Sodom" represents filthiness and wickedness (Genesis 18:20, 21; Jude 7; II Peter 2:6-8). "Egypt" represents oppression.

The jubilant celebration over the death of the two prophets is universal; "people, tribe, language and nation" indicates the fourfold distribution of the human family. Gifts are distributed as at a joyous festival. The death of truth was the cause of public rejoicing, but divine vindication was just around the corner. Remorse was about to replace rejoicing.

Public vilification now gives way to public vindication, The Spirit of life from God causes the dead bones of the witnesses to live, and the spectators are panic stricken. Similarities can be drawn between Israel's dry bones (Ezekiel 37:10-11; Hosea 6:2) and our Lord's resurrection after three days. Christ's ascension was in the presence of His friends (Acts 1:9), as was Elijah's (II Kings 2:11). But the ascension of these two raised witnesses (compare 11:12 with 4:1) is in full view of their enemies.

Now retributive justice quickly falls on the people and the city. An earthquake, called "severe" because of its appalling destruction, causes a tenth of the city to fall and seven thousand people to perish. In the "tenth" we have complete judgment, for "ten" signifies perfection of divine order. In the seven thousand slain we have God's blacklist. These are marked out as deserving of God's righteous judgments. By contrast, we have the seven thousand people in Israel whom God reserved for Himself (I Kings 19:18). In this fixed number of people who are doomed to death we have the two perfect and comprehensive numbers seven and thousand, implying the full and complete destruction of the impenitent.

Summarizing the courageous ministry of the two witnesses, we have them declaring Christ, the rejected One, as the Lord of the whole earth. They testify unsparingly of human wickedness, thereby incurring the hatred of the godless. They proclaim the just character of the Judge, warning the people of righteous retribution in the days to come, decrying the blasphemous claims of the wild beast, and preaching against Jerusalem (which, although holy in God's purpose, had become corrupt and was destroyed).

Of "the survivors" (that is, the spared Israelite inhabitants) it is said that they were filled with godly fear and gave glory to the God of heaven, where the two witnesses had gone. At long last the God of heaven is also acknowledged as the God of the earth.

THIRD WOE—EARTHQUAKE AND HAILSTORM (11:15-19)

Seventh Trumpet Christ Will Reign Forever

Revelation 11:15-19

VERSE 15
Then the seventh angel sounded: And there were loud voices in heaven, saying, "The kingdoms of this word have become the kingdoms of our Lord and of His Christ, and He shall reign forever and ever!"

VERSE 16
And the twenty-four elders who sat before God on their thrones fell on their faces and worshiped God

VERSE 17
saying: "We give You thanks, O Lord God Almighty, The One who is and who was and who is to come, because You have taken Your great power and reigned.

VERSE 18

The nations were angry, and Your wrath has come, And the time of the dead, that they should be judged, And that you should reward Your servants the prophets and the saints, And those who fear your name, small and great, And should destroy those who destroy the earth."

VERSE 19

Then the temple of God was opened in heaven, and the ark of His covenant was seen in His temple. And there were lightnings, noises, thunderings, an earthquake, and great hail.

We now reach the third woe, which is the seventh trumpet. Six is close to seven, in six, but does not reach it. World judgments are complete in six, but by the fulfillment of seven the world kingdoms become Christ's. Six is the number of the world given over to judgment. It is half of twelve, the number of the tribes and apostles, even as three and one-half is half of seven, the divine number for completeness.

The beast had ascended up out of the Abyss to perform his deadly work, and now Christ descends out of heaven to take to Himself His great power as the blessed and only Potentate. What a dramatic scene is presented of God's panorama of future and final events!

In the seventh trumpet angel, some writers see Gabriel, whose name is compound of El ("God") and Geber ("mighty man") and who appropriately announced to Mary the advent of the mighty God-man. It would be fitting for this archangel to announce the final triumph of the Christ of God.

The loud voices in heaven are in contrast to the silence in heaven of 8:1. Exultant praises abound over the setting up of heaven's sovereignty over the earth visibly – when it was invisibly exercised, the earthly rulers rejected it. The anticipation of the kingdom (rather that its actual establishment) causes the heavenly joy in this passage.

The seventh trumpet is akin to the seventh seal in that no immediate judgment is announced. Nothing is recorded as immediately resulting from the trumpet's being blown. We are simply given a summary of the final phases that bring us to the portal of the new creation. The setting up of the world kingdom is treated as a fact: "The kingdom of the world has become the kingdom of our Lord and of His Christ."

Of course, this is the crowning lesson of the Apocalypse. Christ's absolute sovereignty is the sure and glorious outcome of an age-old struggle. He scorned partnership with Satan in ruling the world, and now He is about to exercise

His sovereign rights, and to reign as world emperor. Earth is to enter its last throes of agony. Its millennial morning will dawn with Christ as King over all. His beneficent rule will provide a happy contrast to past and present governmental rule! One universal kingdom will cover the globe, with Christ as the sole reigning Monarch.

Such a sublime prospect demands the adoration of the elders. Profound worship is their response to the heavenly voices. A doxology follows, in which the elders magnify God and Christ for uniting in taking the kingdom. There are seven doxologies in the course of these apocalyptic visions, of which this is one. These are introduced only on occasions of deep interest: 5 12-14; 7:12; 11:15; 12:10-12; 14:2-3; 15:2-4; 19:1-3.

Heaven's wrath will match that of earth (11:18). There is fearful progress in these words, for the unbounded anger of the nations will be destroyed by the divine anger. How petty the nations' impotent anger, standing here side by side with that of omnipotent God! (See Exodus 15:9-16; Psalm 2 for allusions to this double anger.)

The judgment of 11:18 is the judgment of the unbelieving. We are now brought to the conclusion of the kingdom, with the great white throne. Among the many judgments, these four must be kept distinct: the judgment of believers at the "bema" (I Corinthians 3:12-15); the judgment of the nations at the beginning of Christ's reign (Matthew 25:32); and the judgment of the wicked dead at the end of Christ's reign (Revelation 20:11-12).

Rewards are to be bestowed on all God's saints who deserve them. In the kingdom there will be varying degrees and positions of honor. While rest and glory will be for all saints, special crowns will be awarded only to those who have earned them. The faithful believers of every era of church history are to be graciously recompensed.

But retribution awaits all destroyers. Satan, the beast, the false prophet, and all who have followed them are to be recompensed for their wickedness (Daniel 7:14-18; Luke 19:27; Revelation 16:5-7). Destruction overtakes all destroyers.

"Then God's temple in heaven was opened, and within His temple was seen the ark of His covenant" (11:19). This temple is the sign that God is taking up the cause and interests of Israel, and it is in heaven that God is occupied with His people rather than on earth. The ark of His covenant is the token of Jehovah's presence with His earthly people and His unchanging faithfulness toward them. God will remember His covenant with Israel. (This is one of the seven great "openings" in Revelation; the other six are a door is opened in heaven [4:1]; seals are opened [6:1-9]; the abyss is opened [9:2]; the tabernacle of the testimony is opened [15:5]; heaven is opened [19:11]; and books are opened [20:12].)

The trumpet judgments close with judgment action over the whole earth. Here is the storm of divine wrath that has its origin in heaven. Short, sharp, and decisive judgments are indicated by the combination of destructive elements. Natural forces are poured out by their Creator to mete out His righteous wrath upon all who persist in resisting His claims. God now operates in terrible might and majesty.

By the seventh trumpet we learn that warnings of God are perfect and complete, leaving humans without excuse when final and irreversible doom falls upon them.

REVELATION 12

THE WOMAN CLOTHED WITH THE SUN (12:1-2)

VERSE 1

Now a great sign appeared in heaven: a woman clothed with the sun, with the moon under her feet, and on her head a garland of twelve stars.

There appeared a great wonder in heaven. The word "wonder" is the Greek word semeion. It occurs fifty-one times in the New Testament, and forty-eight of those times it is translated "sign."

A woman clothed with the sun, and the moon under her feet, and upon her head a crown of twelve stars. There have been various interpretations as to the identity of this woman. Some say she is the Virgin Mary. As we have seen, most of the symbols used in the Revelation have Old Testament origin. In Genesis 37:9-11, we have a similar description concerning Joseph's dream. The sun is identified as being Jacob; the moon is his mother, Rachael; and the twelve stars are the twelve sons of Jacob. Joseph and his eleven brothers were the twelve patriarchs from whom the twelve tribes of Israel descended. Hence, the "woman clothed with the sun" represents the nation of Israel. Israel throughout the Bible is referred to as a married woman (Isaiah 54:1, 66:7-9; Jeremiah 3:1-25; Hosea 2:1-23; Micah 4:10, and Luke 18:1-18).

VERSE 2
Then being with child, she cried out in labor and in pain to give birth.

She being with child cried. The "child" is the Messiah that was prophesied to come from the nation of Israel (Isaiah 9:6, 7; and Romans 9:5).

And pained to be delivered. This describes the long years in which Israel travailed, awaiting the birth of her Messiah. The history of Israel is one of suffering, and oppression. No nation has been persecuted as Israel has, and survived. Israel's hope over the years was her anticipation of the coming Messiah.

THE GREAT DRAGON (12:3-4)
VERSE 3
And another sign appeared in heaven: behold, a great, fiery red dragon having seven heads and ten horns, and seven diadems on his heads.

There appeared another wonder in heaven. The word "another" is the Greek word allos, and means "another of the same kind." Thus, this wonder is tied to the wonder of the "sun clothed woman."

A great red dragon. The identity of the dragon is explained in verse nine, and also chapter 20, verse two. It is none other than the age-old enemy of God, Satan. He is described as a "red dragon." The word "red" is purros, and means "blood-red." The word "dragon" is drakon and means "a vicious monster." Satan is described here as a vicious monster, covered with the blood of his victims.

Having seven heads. "Seven" is the number of completion. The "head" is used in the Bible as "the source of wisdom or intellect." Here, Satan is seen as being full of wisdom. However, he is not omniscient.

And ten horns. This is probably a reference to Daniel, chapter seven. "Ten is also used to refer to "completion." The "horn," is a symbol of power (Daniel 7:7, 8, 20, 24). Here, Satan is seen as being a powerful ruler.

And seven crowns upon his heads. Satan is not only wise and powerful, but he is the king of virtually all the people who live on this earth. Seven symbolizes that which is complete. The word for "crown" is diadem, and refers to the crown of the king. Jesus acknowledged that the majority of people would follow Satan's rule rather than His own (Matthew 7:13-23). However, even during the Tribulation Period, there will be those who will not follow his rule (Revelation 7).

VERSE 4

His tail drew a third of the stars of heaven and threw them to the earth. And the dragon stood before the woman who was ready to give birth, to devour her Child as soon as it was born.

His tail drew the third part of the stars of heaven. The word for "drew" is suro, and means "to violently drag." The word for "stars" is aster, and is used Metaphorically to describe "the angels" (Job 38:7). The word "stars," here, refers to the angels that rebelled with Satan, and were forced out of heaven. According to Scripture, one-third of the angels in Heaven rebelled (Isaiah 14:12-17; Ezekiel 28:12-19; Luke 10:18; II Peter 2:4, and Jude 6).

And did cast them to the earth. Satan and his fallen angels were cast out of heaven down to the earth's atmosphere. This was the first of four falls of Satan referred to in the Bible (Isaiah 14:12ff).

And the dragon stood before the woman which was ready to be delivered. "Stood" literally means "kept standing."

For to devour her child as soon as it was born. The reason Satan keeps standing before the pregnant woman is to "devour" her newborn child. The word for "devour" is kataphago and means "to consume by eating." Satan's intent over the ages has been to destroy the woman's child, the Messiah. Throughout the Bible, we read of Satan's attempts at this. Abel, the righteous was slain, but God raised up Seth. The trouble between Jacob and Esau was Satan's attempt to eliminate Jacob. Attempts were made by Satan to destroy Moses, the prophets, etc. Haman tried to destroy the entire nation of Israel, and thus the Messiah would not have been born. Satan tried to cause Mary to miscarry through the decree of Caesar (Luke 2:1-6). The trip from Nazareth to Bethlehem would have been extremely difficult for a pregnant woman. After the birth of Jesus, Satan tried to kill the Messiah by causing Herod to slaughter all the male children under the age of two (Mathew 2:16). As Jesus began His earthly ministry, Satan tried to kill Him (Matthew 4:1-11).

Throughout the ministry of Jesus, Satan actively tried to destroy Him.

THE MAN CHILD (12:5-6)

VERSE 5

She bore a male Child who was to rule all nations with a rod of iron. And her Child was caught up to God and His throne.

And she brought forth a man child. The phrase literally means "she bore a son." In God's own time, Israel gave birth to the Messiah, despite Satan's attempts to prevent it (Galatians 4:4).

Who was to rule all nations with a rod of iron. This phrase is taken from Psalm 2:9, and refers to the coming Messiah. This is further evidence that the man-child born of this woman was the Messiah. Jesus will o4 day be the absolute ruler of all nations (Daniel 7:13-14; Ephesians 1:20-22; Philippians 2:9-11, and I Peter 3:2).

And her child was caught up unto God, and to His throne. Here, John mentions the birth of Jesus, and then goes directly to His ascension into Heaven (Mark 16:19-20; Luke 24:49-53, and Acts 1:6-11). Jesus went to Heaven to assume

His throne (Acts 7:55; Romans 8:34, and Hebrews 4:14, 9:24).

VERSE 6
Then the woman fled into the wilderness, where she has a place prepared by God, that they should feed her there one thousand two hundred and sixty days.

And the woman fled into the wilderness. The church age occurs between verses five and six. This is the time between the sixty-ninth and seventieth weeks of Daniel (Daniel 9:24-27). John skips this period because he has already dealt with it in Revelation, chapter two and three. The "woman," as we have seen is Israel. Since Satan has been totally unsuccessful in destroying the male child of the woman, he turns his attention to the woman herself. It should be noted that the woman flees not for the safety of her child, for He has been taken to Heaven, but for her own safety. Satan's wrath has always been vented toward the nation of Israel, but it will intensify during the final three and a half years of the Tribulation Period.

Where she has a place prepared of God. God has promised to preserve His people. He always has a place of refuge prepared for them. God preserved Israel in the wilderness

(Deuteronomy 8:2ff). He preserved the prophet Elijah as he fled to Cherith (I Kings 17:2ff). He preserved the Christ child and Joseph and Mary as they fled to Egypt (Matthew 2:13). The location of the place where Israel will flee during the last three and a half years of the Tribulation Period is not certain. However, Isaiah mentions the city of Sela in the wilderness of Moab as a place of refuge (Isaiah 16:4). Sela is the Hebrew form of the Greek name Petra, meaning "rock." Petra is located about fifty miles south of the Dead Sea. It was the capital of the ancient Edomite Empire. It is situated in a fertile basin at an elevation of 3,800 feet above sea level, and can only be entered through a narrow, twisting gorge, the walls of which rise a thousand feet higher. Petra would be a perfect hideaway for Israel during this period.

A thousand two hundred and threescore days. This number refers to the last three and a half years of the Tribulation Period. During the first three and a half years of the Tribulation, the Antichrist will appear to be the friend of Israel, but he will turn on them during the middle of the Tribulation and try to destroy them.

MICHAEL (12:7-9)

VERSE 7

And war broke out in heaven: Michael and his angels fought with the dragon; and the dragon and his angels fought,

There was war in heaven. This phrase literally means "there came to be war in the heavens." The word "heaven "is ouranos, and refers to the atmosphere. We have already seen that the atmosphere is the place of Satan's domain (Ephesians 2:2).

Michael and his angels fought against the dragon; and the dragon fought and his angels. In chapter twelve, we have already been introduced to three of the characters that will take part in the Tribulation drama, and now in verse seven, we are introduced to the fourth—Michael. As Satan tries to destroy Israel, the armies of heaven under the leadership of Michael, will respond, and there will be war between the angels of God, and the fallen angels of Satan. Michael is the Archangel that is the special guardian of Israel (Daniel 10:13, 21; 12:1; and Jude 9).

VERSE 8

but they did not prevail, nor was a place found for them in heaven any longer.

And prevailed not. Hallejuah! Satan is a defeated foe! God is omnipotent!

Neither was their place found any more in heaven. As a result of this war, Satan is cast from the atmosphere, the place of his kingdom.

VERSE 9

So the great dragon was cast out, that serpent of old, called the Devil and Satan, who deceives the whole world; he was cast to the earth, and his angels were cast out with him.

And the great dragon was cast out. As we have already seen, the dragon is Satan. That old serpent. Again, this is a reference to Satan (Genesis 3:1ff). Called the devil. The word "devil" is diabolos and means "the accuser." And Satan. The word "Satan" is satanas and means "the adversary."

Which deceived the whole world. The phrase literally reads "the deceiver of the whole world." Satan's goal is to blind all men to the truth of God. The word for "world" is oikoumene and refers to "the inhabited world" (Luke 2:1; Revelation 3:10; and 16:14). Satan is such a master of deception, that he can almost "lead astray" the very elect of God (Matthew 24:24).

He was cast out into the earth and his angels were cast out with him. This is the second of the four falls of Satan described in the Bible. We have already seen the first, when he was cast out of Heaven into the atmosphere (Ephesians 2:2). During the idle of the Tribulation Period, as a result of war with Michael, he will be cast down to the earth. The word "earth" is gen, and refers to the "physical earth.

THE LAMB (12:10-17)

VERSE 10

Then I heard a loud voice saying in heaven, "Now salvation, and strength, and the kingdom of our God, and the power of His Christ have come, for the accuser of our brethren, who accused them before our God day and night, has been cast down.

I heard a loud voice saying in heaven. The scene once again shifts from earth to Heaven. The identity of the person speaking is not given. Perhaps it is one of the twenty-four elders.

Now is come salvation. When Satan is cast down to the earth, there is rejoicing in Heaven, for now is come salvation. The word "salvation" is hosoteria, and literally means "the salvation." The idea behind the concept of salvation is "deliverance, preservation and victory."

And strength. The word "strength" is dunomis and means "miraculous power."

And the kingdom of our God. The phrase literally means "the empire of our God," as in Revelation 11:15.

And the power of His Christ. The phrase literally means "the authority given to the anointed one." Jesus said, "All power is given unto Me" (Matthew 28:18; John 17:2). Those in Heaven praise God that deliverance from Satan, the adversary, has come, and God has asserted His miraculous power in establishing His empire, which will be under the authority of His Christ.

For the accuser of our brethren is cast down. "Brethren" refers to those who are saved on earth during the Tribulation Period and still battling against the Devil.

Which accused them before our God day and night Satan is the great "accuser," and he is constantly accusing the brethren before God (Job 1:6ff). "Day and night" is literally "by day and by night." Satan never rests, he is constantly coming before God and saying that we are neither righteous nor worthy.

VERSE 11

"And they overcame him by the blood of the Lamb and by the word of their testimony, and they did not love their lives to the death.

And they overcame him. "They" again refers to those saints still living during the Tribulation Period. The word "overcame" is a legal term. Satan is constantly saying that we are not legally entitled to the blessings of God because we are sinners. But, these saints have a legal defense against his accusations.

By the blood of the Lamb. This legal defense is "the blood of Jesus." We are worthy, not in our own merit, but because of the sacrifice of Jesus (John 1:29; and I Peter 1:18-21).

And by the word of their testimony. Jesus said that no one could be saved unless they openly confess their faith in Him (Matthew 10:32-33; and Luke 12:8-9). We are saved by our confession of Christ, and we live a victorious life over the Devil by confessing Him daily.

And they loved not their lives unto the death. Their first defense against Satan, as we saw, was their acceptance of the sacrifice of Jesus for their sins. The second defense was their faithful confession of Jesus as their Savior and Lord. The third element in their defense against Satan is that they do not put their own lives before their loyalty to Christ. Jesus constantly reminded us that this is the way to victory (Matthew 10:39; 16:25; Mark 8:35; Luke 9:24[1]; 17:33 and John 12:25).

VERSE 12

"Therefore rejoice, 0 heavens, and you who dwell in them! Woe to the inhabitants of the earth and the sea! For the devil has come down to you, having great wrath, because he knows, hat he has a short time."

Therefore rejoice 0 heavens, and you that dwell in them. This points back to verse ten. Because Satan is a defeated foe, the saints of God, already in Heaven, and also those still living during the terrible time of the Tribulation can rejoice. The word "rejoice" means "to make merry."

Woe to the inhabiters of the earth and of the sea. The word "woe" is the typical way of expressing severe lament or grief.

For the devil is come down unto you. That which caused rejoicing among the saints of God, is reason for lament among those who are lost.

Having great wrath. Incensed at his headlong and final expulsion from heaven, and enraged at his defeat at the hands of Michael and his angels, and realizing that he only has three and a half years left (the last half of the Tribulation Period) in which to get revenge, Satan sets out to bring all his wrath to bear upon the inhabiters of earth. "Great wrath" is thumon and means "boiling rage."

Because he knows that he has but a short time. "Short time" is literally "little time." After the Devil's expulsion from his domain in the air, he realizes that little time remains before he is cast into the bottomless pit during the millennial reign of Christ.

VERSE 13

Now when the dragon saw that he had been cast to the earth, he persecuted the woman who gave birth to the male Child.

He persecuted the woman which brought forth the man child. The woman, as we have already seen in verses one and two, is the nation of Israel. Satan has always hated the nation of Israel, and that is why the history of Israel has been one of persecution. However, his hatred and persecution will intensify during these last days of the Tribulation Period.

VERSE 14

But the woman was given two wings of a great eagle, that she might fly into the wilderness to her place, where she is nourished for a time and times and half a time, from the presence of the serpent.

And the woman was given two wings of a great eagle. The eagle in the Bible is often pictured as a means of deliverance since he soars high above the earth (Exodus 19:4; Job 9:26; Proverbs 24:54; and Isaiah 40:31).

That she might fly into the wilderness, into her place. The "place referred to is described in verse six.

For a time, and times and half a time. "Time" equals a "year," "times" equals "two years," and "half a time" equals "half a year." This refers to a three and a half year period.

From the face of the serpent. The "serpent" (Satan will rule the earth during the Tribulation Period. Israel will be protected for three and a half years from the presence of Satan.

VERSE 15

So the serpent spewed water out of his mouth like a flood after the woman, that he might cause her to be carried away by the flood.

The serpent cast out of his mouth. The idea here is that the serpent, Satan, is the source of what is about to occur.

Armies as a flood will go after the woman. As Israel flees to the place God has prepared for her, Satan will send his armies, as a flood, after her to destroy her.

That he might cause her to be carried away by the flood. Satan's intent is plain—he seeks to utterly destroy Israel.

VERSE 16

But the earth helped the Woman, and the earth opened its mouth and swallowed up the flood which the dragon had spewed out of his mouth.

And the earth helped the woman. God will cause some supernatural act of nature to prevent Satan from destroying Israel until I she reaches the wilderness where she will be safe.

VERSE 17

And the dragon was enraged with the woman, and he went to make war with the rest of her offspring, who keep the commandments of God and have the testimony of Jesus Christ.

And the dragon was enraged with the woman. As a result of God's intervention to save Israel, Satan is outraged, and his anger toward Israel intensifies.

And went to make war. The phrase literally mans "went away." After this defeat, Satan will retreat and make further "war plans."

With the rest of her offspring, who keep the commandments of God and have the testimony of Jesus Christ. Having been unsuccessful in destroying the nation of Israel, Satan now seeks out her "offspring who keep the commandments of God and have the testimony of Jesus Christ." This is a reference to those Jews who will accept Jesus as their Savior during the Tribulation Period. They will be special targets of Satan's' anger.

REVELATION 13

THE ANTICHRIST (13:1-10)

VERSE 1

Then I stood on the sand of the sea. And I saw a beast rising up out of the sea, having seven heads and ten horns, and on his horns ten crowns, and on his heads a blasphemous name.

I stood on the sand of the sea and saw a beast rise up out of the sea. In the Greek text the phrase "I stood on the sand of the sea" literally reads "he stood upon the sand of the sea," and belongs to the twelfth chapter. In the last verse of chapter twelve, we read where the dragon (Satan) was wroth, and went to make war. In chapter thirteen, verse one, he stands upon the sands of the sea and calls out of the raging sea a beast that is the Antichrist. The "sea" is commonly used in the Bible to describe "the Gentile nations of the world" (Psalms 6:7; Isaiah 9:5; Jeremiah 51:42; and Daniel 7:2). The word "beast" is therion and means a vicious wild beast. This beast is the Antichrist and he arises out of the Gentile nations of the world. In Daniel he is referred to as the "little horn" (Daniel 7:8, 20, 21, 24, 25), the "willful King" (Daniel 11:36), and the "coming prince" (Daniel 9:26). In II Thessalonians chapter two he is called the "man of sin."

Having seven heads and ten horns. A similar description is given in Daniel 7:7-8. In Revelation 17:9-14 the seven heads and ten horns are explained. The "seven" heads are "seven mountains" upon which the kingdom of the Antichrist will be seated. In the Old Testament, as here, "mountains" are often used to refer to world powers or empires (Isaiah 2:2; Jeremiah 51:25; and Daniel 2:35). In Revelation 17, verse 10, John says that five of these empires have already fallen (Egypt, Assyria, Babylon, Medo—Persia, and Greece as identified in Daniel 7), one now is (the Roman Empire of John's day), and the other is not yet come (The Revived Roman Empire of the Antichrist). The "ten horns" are ten kings which have no kingdom as yet (a confederation of ten nations—a Revived Roman Empire—from which the Antichrist will rule the world).

Upon his horns ten crowns. "Ten" is the number that symbolizes completion. The word "crowns" is diadem, and refers to the crown of the reigning monarch. This mighty confederation of ten nations under the Antichrist will rule the whole world.

And upon his heads the name of blasphemy. The word "blasphemy" is blasphemed, and means to speak slanderously with the intent of injury.

VERSE 2

Now the beast which I saw was like a leopard, his feet were like the feet of a bear, and his mouth like the mouth of a lion. The dragon gave him his power, his throne, and great authority.

The beast which I saw was like unto. The Antichrist and his kingdom will resemble the mighty world empires of old.

A leopard. In Daniel 7:6, the leopard represented the swiftness of the kingdom of Greece under Alexander the Great.

His feet were as the feet of a bear. In Daniel 7:5, the bear represented the strength of the Medo—Persian Empire.

His mouth as the mouth of a lion. In Daniel 7:4, the lion represented the majesty and power of the great Babylonian Empire.

And the dragon gave him his power. In addition to the kingdom of the Antichrist having the combined powers of the world empires of old, it is also super naturally empowered by Satan. This will be the greatest empire the world has ever known.

And his seat and great authority. The word "seat" is thronos and means throne. The word "authority" is exousia and means "ability or strength with which one is endued." The Antichrist will be endued with strength by Satan.

VERSE 3
And I saw one of his heads as if it had been mortally wounded, and his deadly wound was healed. And all the world marveled and followed the beast.

And I saw one of his heads as if it had been wounded by death. Remember, whatever God does, Satan imitates. We have already seen his counterfeit trinity. Now, he stages a fake death and resurrection of his Antichrist in order to deceive the world into following him. We know that his death and resurrection is fake, because only God has the power of life and death (Genesis 2:7; Job 2:3-6).

And all the world marveled and followed the beast. "Deadly wound" is literally "death-stroke." The Antichrist will appear to be resurrected from the dead.

And all the world marveled and followed the beast. The whole world will be amazed at the resurrection of their great leader—the Antichrist.

VERSE 4

So they worshiped the dragon who gave authority to the beast; and they worshiped the beast, saying, "Who is like the beast? Who is able to make war with him?"

They worshiped the dragon who gave authority to the beast. The resurrection of the Antichrist will cause the peoples of the world to worship (proskuneo which means to pay homage or make obeisance to) the dragon—Satan. It is obvious to them that the means by which the Antichrist is resurrected is the power of Satan.

And they worshiped the beast. They also worship the Antichrist saying "who is like unto the beast?" Their amazement and wonder is shown in their exclamation, "Who can compare with the Antichrist!"

Who is able to make war with him? Worship of the Devil and the Antichrist is justified purely on the ground of brute force. It is the doctrine of Nietzschi that "might makes right." The Antichrist will be admired for his military might.

VERSE 5

And he was given a mouth speaking great things and blasphemies, and he was given authority to continue for forty-two months.

And he was given. Again it is plain that the source of the Antichrist's power is the dragon (Satan).

A mouth speaking great things and blasphemies. In Daniel 7:8, a similar description is given. The Antichrist will be given the knowledge, and the ability to deliver forceful speeches, filled with promises and propaganda. In addition to his hellish propaganda, his speeches will be filled with blasphemy (slanderous speech intended to injure God's reputation).

And authority was given to him to continue for forty-two months. This refers to the last three and a half years of the Tribulation Period when the Antichrist will almost have "unhindered power."

VERSE 6

Then he opened his mouth in blasphemy against God, to blaspheme His name, His tabernacle, and those who dwell in heaven.

Then he opened his mouth in blasphemy against God. The purpose of the blasphemous speech of the Antichrist is to discredit God.

To blaspheme His name. In Bible days, the name of a person was supposed to represent their character or nature. The Antichrist is intent on slandering the character of God.

His tabernacle. The Antichrist will not only blaspheme God's character, but also His house of worship. He will speak slanderous remarks against the true worship of God.

And those who dwell in heaven. Even the saints in Heaven will not be exempt from his slander. This may be a reference to those who were saved during the Tribulation Period, killed by the Antichrist and now in Heaven under the altar (Revelation 6:9-11). He may say something like this, "Look at these people who served God, I killed them, and now they are no more." We must always remember that Satan hates God, and therefore, he hates those who belong to God.

VERSE 7

It was granted to him to make war with the saints and to overcome them. And authority was given him over every tribe, tongue, and nation.

It was granted to him to make war with the saints. This is the fifth time in chapter thirteen that we are reminded that the Antichrist derives his power from Satan. During the last three and a half years of the Tribulation Period, he makes war with the saints on earth that have been saved (Revelation 6:9). This will be Satan's last fling at the people of God.

To overcome them. The saints on earth will be no match for the mightiest empire the world has ever known. They will be slaughtered.

And authority was given him. This is the sixth time in chapter thirteen that we are told that the power of the Antichrist is not his own.

Over every tribe, tongue, and nation. This refers to the whole world. The word "kindred DUVI" is phulg and means a group of people united by kinship or habitation—a clan or tribe. "Tongues" refers to groups that speak the same language. "Nations" refers to specific groups of people.

VERSE 8
All who dwell on the earth will worship him, whose names have not been written in the Book of Life of the Lamb slain from the foundation of the world.

All who dwell on the earth will worship him. The Antichrist will achieve what many have desired over the ages—worldwide rule.

Whose names have not been written in the Book of Life. While his rule will be worldwide, it will not be universal. In chapter seven, we saw that there will be 144,000 Jews saved, and also a multitude of Gentiles which cannot be numbered. However, the only exception to is rule will be these whose names are written in the Book of Life.

Of the Lamb slain from the foundation of the world. The only one able to give us eternal life in Jesus, the Lamb of God who was ordained to be slain even before the world was formed.

VERSE 9
If anyone has an ear, let him hear.

Let him hear. Even in the midst of this dark hour, God's invitation is issued just as it was during the church age (Revelation2-3).

VERSE 10
He who leads into captivity shall go into captivity; he who kills with the sword must be killed with the sword. Here is the patience and the faith of the saints.

He who leads into captivity shall go into captivity. This is God's promise of Divine Retribution. The Antichrist who has led countless multitudes into captivity will, in God's time, be taken captive (Revelation 19:20).

He who kills with the sword must be killed with the sword. This is reminiscent of the words of Jesus in Matthew 26:52. The Antichrist will come to a violent end. In Revelation 19:20, he will be "cast alive" into the Lake of Fire. The Greek word "cast" is hallo and means "to violently hurl down."

Here is the patience and the faith of the saints. The word "patience" is hupomone and means to "abide under, or to undergird." The word "faith" is pistis, and here should be rendered more properly "faithfulness of fidelity." The thing that undergirds and keeps the Tribulation saints (and the saints of all ages) going, is their knowledge that in the end, God will make all things right. Those who lead into captivity will be taken captive, and those who kill with the sword will be killed by the sword! "Vengeance is mine says the Lord, I will repay" (Romans 12:19).

THE FALSE PROPHET (13:11-18)

VERSE 11

Then I saw another beast coming up out of the earth, and he had two horns like a lamb and spoke like a dragon.

Then I saw another beast coming up out of the earth. After having been introduced to the Antichrist in the first ten verses, we are now introduced to the second beast. The word "another" is allos and means "another of the same kind." The second beast is similar to the first one. The second beast is the "False Prophet" (Revelation 19:20), the third person of the Satanic Trinity. The dragon (Satan) is the antithesis of God the Father, who is the source of all good. Satan is the source of all evil. The Antichrist is the antithesis of Jesus who is the Son of God. The Antichrist is the son of perdition (II Thessalonians 2:3). The False Prophet is the antithesis of the Holy Spirit, who is the "Spirit of Truth" (John 14:17), and who causes people to worship Jesus. The False Prophet will cause the peoples of the world to worship the Antichrist. The Antichrist will arise from the "sea," which represents the restlessness of the Gentile nations. The False Prophet will arise from the earth. The "earth" is not as unstable as the restless "sea." The idea may be that the False Prophet will appear on the scene after the Antichrist has apparently brought a degree of stability to the chaotic world during the first three and a half years of the Tribulation Period.

And he had two horns like a lamb and spoke like a dragon. The False Prophet will be the world leader of an apostate religion which will glorify the Antichrist. He had "two horns like a lamb." Again, Satan is seen as the great imitator. Jesus came as the "Lamb of God" (John1:29). The False Prophet appears to be a lamb (weak and innocent), but in reality he is as vile as the dragon (Satan). The true prophet speaks the "truth" of God, but this prophet is "false" (pseudo literally "lying"), and speaks the "lies" of the Devil (John 8:44).

VERSE 12

And he exercises all the authority of the first beast in his presence, and causes the earth and those who dwell in it to worship the first beast, whose deadly wound was healed.

He exercises all the authority of the first beast. T is second beast has the same power as the Antichrist. The source of his power is a so the dragon (Satan).

In his presence. This also seems to suggest that the False Prophet will appear on the scene after the Antichrist.

And cause the earth and those who dwell in it to worship the first beast. Just as the Holy Spirit—the Spirit of Truth—was sent to earth to point men to Jesus, the False Prophet comes to point men to the Antichrist.

VERSE 13

He performs great signs, so that he even makes fire come down from heaven on the earth in the sight of men.

He performs great signs. The False Prophet is empowered by Satan to perform many wondrous miracles, just like the Antichrist (Revelation 13:3).

So that he even makes fire come down from heaven. Again, Satan is the great imitator. In chapter eleven, we saw that God will send two witnesses to earth during the last three and a half years of the Tribulation Period, to preach. These witnesses will probably be Moses and Elijah, and they will have the power to destroy their enemies with fire that proceeds from their mouth. Again, Satan imitates what God does (Mark 1:22 and II Thessalonians 2:9). He calls forth his False Prophet, and empowers him to call fire down from the heavens. This particular sign was thought to be evidence that a person had the approval of the "true" God (I Kings 18:38; II Kings 1:10; and Luke 9:54).

VERSE 14

And he deceives those who dwell on the earth by those signs which he was granted to do in the sight of the beast, telling those who dwell on the earth to make an image to the beast who was wounded by the sword and lived.

And he deceives those who dwell on the earth. The great ability of the Antichrist to deceive the world will be enhanced by the fact that God Himself will cause them to have "strong delusion, that they should believe a lie" (II Thessalonians 2:1-11).

By those signs. Signs and wonders have always appealed to the natural man (II Thessalonians 2:9). The False Prophet will perform many miracles and thereby cause the peoples of earth to worship the Antichrist.

Telling those who dwell on earth to make an image to the beast. This is a reference to emperor worship. The False Prophet will lead the peoples of earth to not only follow the Antichrist as King, but to recognize him as God. This "image" (statue) will probably be built in the Temple which the Antichrist helps the Jews rebuild during the first half of the Tribulation Period.

VERSE 15

He was granted power to give breath to the image of the beast, that the image of the beast should both speak and cause as many as would not worship the image of the beast to be killed.

He was granted power to give breath to the image of the beast. The False Prophet, after leading the people to build this image of the Antichrist, will perform another miracle and cause "life" (pneuma literally "breath") to come into it. Again, this is an attempt by Satan's part to imitate God. In the beginning, God took the dust of the earth and created man, after which He breathed into him the "breath" (pneuma) of life." During the Tribulation Period, God will breathe life back into the two slain witnesses (Revelation 7). During the Tribulation Period, Satan will create an image which will appear to have life, but it will not, for only God has the power to create life. This "image" will be given the ability to speak and cause all who do not worship the Beast (Antichrist) to be killed.

VERSE 16

He causes all, both small and great, rich and poor, free and slave, to receive a mark on their right hand or on their foreheads,

He causes all ... to receive a mark. The False Prophet will also cause all the followers of the Antichrist to receive a "mark." The word "mark" is charagma and means "a stamp, or impression." The Antichrist will give everyone a number which will include his own number-666.

On their right hand or on their forehead. The location of the mark is given. Both the hand and the forehead are easily visible. Today, we have the ability to inscribe an invisible code that can be scanned electronically, so this should not seem farfetched at all.

VERSE 17

and that no one may buy or sell except one who has the mark or the name of the beast, or the number of his name.

No one may buy or sell except one who has the mark. The purpose of the mark will be a very practical one. Only those who have this mark, evidence that they are a part of the Antichrist's empire, will be able to buy or sell. Those who refuse the mark will be considered a traitor and will either be killed, or left to starve to death.

The name of the beast, or the number of his name. The name and the number are the same-666.

VERSE 18

Here is wisdom. Let him who has understanding calculate the number of the beast, for it is the number of a man: His number is six hundred and sixty-six.

Here is wisdom. Let him who has understanding calculate the number of the beast. If a person is wise, they will evaluate the number of the Beast. At first look, it may appear to be innocent, and merely a means whereby one can buy and sell. But God says, before you receive this mark, think about it. The idea here is to give it careful consideration.

For it is the number of a man: his number is six hundred and sixty-six. The number "six" is used in the Bible to represent "man." The number "three" is used to represent the "Trinity of God." Hence, three sixes, or six raised to the third power, signify the attempt of a man, The Antichrist, to be God. The Antichrist will be the closest that man has ever come to being God. The False Prophet will deceive the world into believing that the Antichrist is God. But, even though he will be the most powerful ruler the world has ever seen and have the largest empire and the most wealth, he is still just a man! It is true that he is Satan's masterpiece, but he is still just a man.

It is later that we think! The reign of this world dictator is upon the horizon.

REVELATION 14

VERSE BY VERSE

THE 144,000 ON MOUNT ZION (14:1-5)

VERSE 1

Then I looked, and behold, a Lamb standing on Mount Zion,
and with Him one hundred and forty-four thousand, having
His Father's name written on their foreheads.

Then I looked. This phrase occurs ten times in the book of
Revelation, and every time it does, it is followed by some
glorious event.

Behold, a Lamb standing on Mount Zion. We have already
been introduced to the "Lamb" in chapter five. He is the
"Lion of the Tribe of Judah," the "Root of David," our
blessed "Lord Jesus Christ." John sees Jesus standing on
Mount (Sion KJV) Zion. The Mount Zion here is probably
the Heavenly one—New Jerusalem (Hebrews 12:22-24)—
not the earthly Jerusalem.

And with Him one hundred and forty-four thousand.
Beginning in chapter twelve, we have been given a
description of six personalities that will play an important
role in the Tribulation drama. We have now come to the

seventh, the 144,000 Jews that were sealed by God in chapter seven. Here we meet them again, at the end of the Tribulation Period. It is encouraging to note that not one of them has been lost, even though they lived during the darkest days this world has ever known. They were persecuted by the Antichrist, but God preserved them all.

Having His Father's name written on their foreheads. These 144,000 have the name of God upon their foreheads as seen in Revelation 3:12 and 22:4, in place of the Mark of the Beast (Revelation 13:16, and 1:21).

VERSE 2

And I heard a voice from heaven, like the voice of many waters, and like the voice of loud thunder. And I heard the sound of harpists playing their harps.

I heard a voice from heaven, like the voice of many waters. The voice is that of the Lord Jesus Christ (Revelation 1:15).

And like the voice of loud thunder. This phrase describes the might and power of the voice.

And I heard the sound of harpists playing their harps. In addition to the voice of the Lord Jesus, John hears the sound of harpists. The identity of the harpists is not given here;

however, they appear to be the martyred saints of God that were killed by the Antichrist during the Tribulation Period (Revelation 6:9; 7:14; and 15:2). The "harp" was the instrument of praise. The voice of Jesus is accompanied by the beautiful music of the harpists as they praise God.

VERSE 3

They sang as it were a new song before the throne, before the four living creatures, and the elders; and no one could learn that song except the hundred and forty-four thousand who were redeemed from the earth.

They sang as it were a new song before the throne. "They" refers to the martyred saints who were playing the harps. They sing a "new song." There are two Greek words for "new." The word neos means "new in time." The word kainos means "new in character or kind." The word used to describe the song the elders sang is kainos and means a new kind of song. There's never been a song like this one before. During Bible times, new songs of praise were needed to express gratitude for new acts of God's mercy (Psalms 33:3; 40:3; 96:1; and Isaiah 42:10). When the Lamb reclaimed the forfeited inheritance in chapter five, verse nine, the twenty-four elders sang a "new song." Now the saints martyred during the Tribulation Period sing this "new song."

Before the four living creatures, and the elders. The Tribulation martyrs sing their "new song" in the presence of God ("the Throne"), the angels ("the Four Beasts"), and those saved under the Old Testament, and New Testament periods ("The Elders").

No one could learn that song except the hundred and forty-four thousand who were redeemed from the earth. As the martyred saints sing the "new song," the 144,000 join in. Only those who have been redeemed can join in the singing of this "new song," for this is a song sung from the heart of one who has experienced the marvelous grace and mighty deliverance of Almighty God. The "new song," is described in Revelation 15:3. It contains two stanzas. The first is the Song of Moses, which was a song of deliverance from earthly enemies (Exodus 15). The second stanza is the Song of the Lamb, which is a song of salvation through the grace of God.

VERSE 4

These are the ones who were not defiled with women, for they are virgins. These are the ones who follow the Lamb wherever He goes. These were redeemed from among men, being first fruits to God and to the Lamb.

These are the ones. In verses four and five, we are given a description of the 144,000 who joined in the singing of the "new song."

Not defiled with women, for they are virgins. This description does not mean that they were unmarried. The New Testament exalts marriage, and this passage should not be construed as degrading it (I Timothy 4:3 and Hebrews 13:4). The word "defile" is moluno and means "to soil, or stain." The 144,000 did not stain their lives with sexual immorality which will be common during the Tribulation Period (Revelation 9:21; 14:8). They are "virgins." "Virgins" is the word parthenos and means "those, either male or female, who are chaste and pure." From these phrases, it is evident that these people have remained pure and lived holy lives in the midst of an ungodly generation.

These are the ones who follow the Lamb wherever He goes. The Christian life is one of following the Lamb of God (Mark 2:14; 10:21; Luke 9:59; John 1:43; 21:19; I Peter 2:21; and I John 2:6). The believer is to follow Jesus wherever He leads, and these did.

These were redeemed from among men. The 144,000 were "redeemed" or saved from among the multitudes living on earth during the Tribulation Period.

Being first fruits to God and to the Lamb. These are the "first fruits" that have been saved by God and the Lamb. The "first fruits" were the first to appear, but, more importantly, were evidence that more fruit was coming. The 144,000 Jews were the first to be sealed by God during the Tribulation, but they were not all that would be saved. In chapter seven, verse nine, we are told that a great multitude which could not be numbered was also saved.

VERSE 5

And in their mouth was found no deceit, for they are without fault before the throne of God.

And in their mouth was found no deceit (guile KJV). The word "guile" is pseudos, and means "a lie, or that which is false." While the "False Prophet" will be covering the earth with lies, the true prophets of God will speak the truth of God.

For they are without fault. These 144,000 have been redeemed by God, remained chaste and holy in the midst of an unholy world, faithfully followed Jesus, preached the truth of God, and now stand before the Throne of God without "fault." The word "fault" is amomos, and is the word that was used to describe the "animal which was without spot or blemish and fit to be used as a sacrifice unto God." This word is often used to describe the Christian (Ephesians 5:1-4, 27; and Colossians 1:22). The 144,000 stand before God's Throne as a worthy offering unto Him.

THE MESSAGE OF THE FIRST ANGEL (14:6-7)

VERSE 6

Then I saw another angel flying in the midst of heaven, having the everlasting gospel to preach to those who dwell on the earth--to every nation, tribe, tongue, and people--

I saw another angel flying in the midst of heaven. After having been introduced to the seven primary characters of the Tribulation drama (Revelation 12:1-14:5), we are now given seven messages from seven angels (Revelation 14:6-20). You remember, from chapter two that the word "angel" is the word angelos, and means "messenger." Sometimes in the Bible, the word refers to "heavenly messengers," and other times "earthly messengers."

Having the everlasting gospel to preach. The first messenger appears to be a heavenly one. However, some believe that the "angel" here is a satellite that will be used to beam the Gospel to all the world. Often times angels deliver messages from Heaven to those on earth. However, it is interesting to note that this is the first time in the Bible that we find an angel preaching the "Gospel." The "Gospel" is the "good news" and contains three elements according to the apostle Paul (I Corinthians 15:14). This "Gospel" is everlasting." It forever remains the same, and will forever endure.

To every nation, tribe, tongue, and people. This refers to the whole world. The word "people" refers to masses without regard to their nationality. The word "kindred" (KJV) is phulg and means a group of people united by kinship or habitation—a clan or tribe. "Tongues" refers to groups that speak the same language. "Nations" refers to specific groups of people.

VERSE 7
saying with a loud voice, "Fear God and give glory to Him, for the hour of His judgment has come; and worship Him who made heaven and earth, the sea and springs of water."

Saying with a loud voice. The message will be proclaimed loud and clear for all to hear.

Fear God and give glory to Him. After the angel delivers the Gospel, he concludes with an invitation, which is "fear God, and give glory to Him." The word "fear" is phobos, and means "a reverential fear that one has of displeasing God." The phrase "give glory to Him" means "to worship Him." The invitation of the angel is to fear God and worship Him.

For the hour of His judgment has come. The angel's plea is to turn to God, and escape His judgment which literally "has already come" upon earth.

Worship Him who made heaven and earth, the sea and springs of water. They are to worship the true God, the Creator of all that there is.

THE MESSAGE OF THE SECOND ANGEL (14:8)

VERSE 8
And another angel followed, saying, "Babylon is fallen, is fallen, that great city, because she has made all nations drink of the wine of the wrath of her fornication."

Another angel followed. The word "another" is allos, and means another of the same kind. The second messenger is similar to the first one.

Saying, Babylon is fallen. Babylon was viewed with special disfavor by the Jews due to the humiliation and persecution of the seventy years of captivity. Babylon was the center of gross immorality and idolatry. During the first century, the Christians referred to Rome, the capital city of the Roman Empire, as the new Babylon, because of its similarity to the old one (oppressive, corrupt, and immoral.) Many Bible scholars believe that the Babylon described in the book of Revelation will be the current city of Rome. The ancient city of Babylon was founded by Nimrod (Genesis 10:10), and it reached its greatest glory under Nebuchadnezzar about 604-562 B.C. The historian Herodotus described the city as being 15 miles square, surrounded by a brick wall 87 feet thick and 350 feet high. Atop that wall were 250 watchtowers, and a roadway wide enough to accommodate six chariots driven abreast. This outside wall was surrounded by a deep moat, filled with water from the Euphrates River. A second wall was located inside this first wall. The city was virtually impregnable. According to the book of Revelation, the Antichrist will rule the world from a capital city that will be similar to ancient Babylon. The glory of the Antichrist's Babylon will exceed that of the ancient city. However, the second angel pronounces its doom. "Is fallen" is literally "fell." The great capital, from which the Antichrist will rule the world, will be destroyed.

Because she has made all nations drink of the wine of the wrath of her fornication. This description is probably taken from Jeremiah 25:15. Babylon will seduce all the nations of the world to become a part of her system, but the angel says that they are actually becoming a part of the wrath of God that will come upon her because of her wickedness.

THE MESSAGE OF THE THIRD ANGEL (14:9-12)

VERSE 9

Then a third angel followed them, saying with a loud voice, "If anyone worships the beast and his image, and receives his mark on his forehead or on his hand.

Then a third angel followed them, saying. We now hear the message of the third angel. It is proclaimed in an unmistakably clear manner.

If anyone worships the beast. The "beast" is the Antichrist.

His image refers to the image of the Antichrist that will be constructed by the False Prophet (Revelation 13:14-15).

And receives his mark on his forehead or on his hand. The mark is the number 666 (Revelation 13:17-18).

VERSE 10

"he himself shall also drink of the wine of the wrath of God, which is poured out full strength into the cup of His indignation. He shall be tormented with fire and brimstone in the presence of the holy angels and in the presence of the Lamb.

He himself shall also drink of the wine of the wrath of God. The third angel gives a stern warning. If anyone becomes a part of the Antichrist's system, they will become the object of God's wrath.

Which is poured out full strength. The wine of God's wrath will not be diluted; it will be full-strength. The fury of God's anger against sin has been held back over the ages by His great mercy, but during the Tribulation Period, it will be released.

Into the cup of His indignation. In Bible days, a king would take a cup of poison, and hand it to a condemned prisoner to drink as a means of execution. This is the picture here. God is going to give those who become a part of the Antichrist's system a cup to drink. It will not be filled with poison, but rather the white-hot wrath of Almighty God.

He shall be tormented with fire and brimstone. The instruments of this judgment are the instruments of hell and the lake of fire (Revelation 20:10). Fire and brimstone are often seen as the instruments of God's awful judgment (Genesis 19:24; Isaiah 30:33 and Ezekiel 38:22).

In the presence of the holy angels and in the presence of the Lamb. In Luke 16, when the rich man died and went to Hell, he saw Abraham and Lazarus in the Paradise of God. Part of the punishment of the wicked will be the consciousness of what they have missed—eternity in the presence of God.

VERSE 11

"And the smoke of their torment ascends forever and ever; and they have no rest day or night, who worship the beast and his image, and whoever receives the mark of his name."

The smoke of their torment ascends forever and ever. Their torment will never cease. They will be tormented eternally. The phrase used is the strongest Greek phrase that can be used to describe eternity. It literally means "unto the age of the ages."

They have no rest day or night. The word "rest" is anapausis, and means "a time of refreshment." It is the word commonly used for the "Sabbath Day." There will be no refreshment for those who are the objects of God's wrath.

VERSE 12

Here is the patience of the saints; here are those who keep the commandments of God and the faith of Jesus.

Here is the patience of the saints. The word "patience" is hupomone and means to "abide under," or to "undergird." The thing that undergirds the saints of God (those whose faith is in Jesus and who obey His commandments) is the knowledge that in the end God will make all things right. He will judge the wicked, and vindicate the righteous.

THE MESSAGE OF THE FOURTH ANGEL (14:13-14)

VERSE 13

Then I heard a voice from heaven saying to me, "Write: 'Blessed are the dead who die in the Lord from now on.'" "Yes," says the Spirit, "that they may rest from their labors, and their works follow them."

Then I heard a voice from heaven saying. The fourth messenger now speaks.

Blessed are the dead who die in the Lord from now on. This message applies specifically to those who will be killed by the Antichrist during the Tribulation Period, but also applies to all who die in the Lord. Here John gives us additional information concerning the condition of the saved dead. They are called "blessed." The word "blessed" is makarios and means to "pronounce happy because one has abundance."

That they may rest from their labors. The wicked have no rest from their punishment (Revelation 14:11). But, the righteous "rest" (anapauo) from their "labors." The word "labor" is kopos, and means "a striking or beating that results in weariness." In this life, we are oppressed on every hand, but for the child of God, there is a day coming when we will have rest (II Timothy 4:6-8). This does not mean that we will not be active, for the Scripture teaches that the saints will rule the world (Revelation 5:20). it means that there will be no fatigue or weariness in what we do.

And their works follow them. Those who die in the Lord are "rejoicing," "resting," and "rewarded." The works that we do for Jesus will one day be rewarded at the Judgment Seat of Christ (I Corinthians 3:11-15).

VERSE 14

Then I looked, and behold, a white cloud, and on the cloud sat One like the Son of Man, having on His head a golden crown, and in His hand a sharp sickle.

Then I looked and behold a white cloud. "Clouds" were thought to be "vehicles of deity."

On the cloud sat One like the Son of Man. "The Son of Man" (Jesus) is the one who John sees coming in the clouds. This is a reference to the Second Coming of Christ (Revelation 19:11-16), not the Rapture of the church (I Thessalonians 3:1318 and Revelation 4:1).

Having on His head a golden crown. Jesus is wearing the stephanos here, not the diadem. The diadem is the crown of the king. The stephanos is the victor's crown, or the crown of the conqueror. Here Jesus is coming back to earth to conquer, and to be victor.

And in His hand a sharp sickle. The "sickle" was the instrument used to reap the harvest of grain. Jesus is coming as the victor, to reap the harvest of earth (Joel 3:12-13;

Matthew 9:38; John 4:35-38 and Hebrews 9:28). The harvest only comes at the end, and the end time has now come.

THE MESSAGE OF THE FIFTH ANGEL (14:15-16)

VERSE 15

And another angel came out of the temple, crying with a loud voice to Him who sat on the cloud, "Thrust in Your sickle and reap, for the time has come for You to reap, for the harvest of the earth is ripe."

And another angel came out of the temple. The fifth angel is about to speak. He comes from the "temple" of God in Heaven.

Crying with a loud voice to Him who sat on the cloud. The angel relays a message to Jesus from the temple.

Thrust in Your sickle and reap. The message which the angel gives to Jesus is "begin the harvest, for the time is right." The message is obviously coming from God the Father, for Jesus said that He is the one who determines when time shall come to an end (Acts 1:7).

For the harvest of the earth is ripe. The word "ripe" is akmazo and means "overripe, or dried." It refers to a harvest that has been left as long as it possibly can without being lost. This illustrates God's great mercy. God has waited as long as He possibly can to begin the final harvest (II Peter 3:9).

VERSE 16
So He who sat on the cloud thrust in His sickle on the earth, and the earth was reaped.

So He who sat on the cloud. As we have seen, "He" is the Lord Jesus. In Matthew thirteen, in the parable of the wheat and the tares, Jesus is seen as the "sower," here He is the "reaper."

THE MESSAGE OF THE SIXTH ANGEL (14:17)

VERSE 17
Then another angel came out of the temple which is in heaven, he also having a sharp sickle.

Then another angel came out of the temple. This is the sixth angelic messenger. He, as did the fifth, comes from the Temple where God dwells.

He also having a sharp sickle. This message of this angel is not verbal, but rather visual. He is seen having a sharp sickle, just as the Lord Jesus did.

THE MESSAGE OF THE SEVENTH ANGEL (14:18-20)

VERSE 18

And another angel came out from the altar, who had power over fire, and he cried with a loud cry to him who had the sharp sickle, saying, "Thrust in your sharp sickle and gather the clusters of the vine of the earth, for her grapes are fully ripe."

And another angel came out from the altar. The seventh and final angel comes from the "altar." This is probably a reference to the "brazen altar" which was the altar of judgment.

Who had power over fire. The brazen altar was the altar where the sacrifices were consumed by fire.

He cried with a loud cry to him who had the sharp sickle. The seventh angel cried out to the sixth angel that had the sharp sickle.

Thrust in your sharp sickle. The word "thrust" is the word ballo and means to throw violently. This refers to the viciousness of the harvest. The day of mercy is past!

And gather the clusters of the vine of the earth. The saints of God are referred to as the "vine of Jesus Christ" (John 15:1-6). In contrast, the lost are referred to as the "vine of the earth."

For her grapes are fully ripe. The word used here for "ripe" is ekmasan, and means "to be at the prime, or fully ripe." Again we are reminded of the great mercy that God has toward mankind. He has waited as long as possible.

VERSE 19
So the angel thrust his sickle into the earth and gathered the vine of the earth, and threw it into the great winepress of the wrath of God.

So the angel thrust his sickle. The sixth angel obeys the command of the seventh angel.

And threw it into the great winepress of the wrath of God. After the angel harvests the vine of the earth, he casts it into the great winepress. The imagery here is clear. In Bible days, after the grapes were harvested, they were put into the winepress. The winepress was a great vat where the grapes were dumped, and the oxen pulled a wheel that pressed all the juice out of the grapes. This juice was then used to make wine. The wicked that have been harvested by the angel are thrown into the winepress of God's wrath.

VERSE 20

And the winepress was trampled outside the city, and blood came out of the winepress, up to the horses' bridles, for one thousand six hundred furlongs.

And the winepress was trampled outside the city. The winepress was usually located outside the city (Hebrews 12:13).

And blood came out of the winepress. The result is not grape juice, but blood. The end product of God's crushing judgment is the death of the wicked.

Up to the horses' bridles. In this final judgment of God, the blood will flow and be as deep as the horse's bridle, about four to five feet deep.

For one thousand six hundred furlongs. The word "furlong" is stadion, and was the length of the Roman stadium, about one-eighth of a mile. The blood will cover an area of about two hundred miles. This distance would cover the entire length of Palestine. The result of God's judgment will be a carnage that will cover an area of about 200 miles, and the blood will be about four feet deep. With this vivid description of God's final judgment, the parenthesis that began in chapter twelve comes to a close. In this parenthesis we have been introduced to seven personalities that will play an important role in the Tribulation drama, and seven angelic messengers. In chapter fifteen, we resume the Seventh Trumpet which introduces the Seven Vials (bowls) of God's wrath.

REVELATION 15

PREPARATION FOR THE VIALS (15:1-8)

VERSE 1

Then I saw another sign in heaven, great and marvelous: seven angels having the seven last plagues, for in them the wrath of God is complete.

Then I saw another sign in heaven, great and marvelous. This is the third great "sign" that John saw in the Revelation. The first was the "woman clothed in the sun" (12:1), and the second was the "great red dragon" (12:3). The word "sign" is semeion, and means "wonder." The word "marvelous" is thauma, and means "to gaze in amazement." The "sign" was so "amazing," that John had to gaze at it to be sure he could believe what he saw.

Seven angels having the seven last plagues. These are not demons, but angels of God. These angels have the concluding "plagues" of God's judgment upon the earth. The word "plague" is plege and means "to smite, strike, or wound."

For in them the wrath of God is complete. The words "filled up" (KW) are etelesthe and mean "to complete." The seven vials will complete the wrath of God poured out during the Tribulation Period.

VERSE 2

And I saw something like a sea of glass mingled with fire, and those who have the victory over the beast, over his image and over his mark and over the number of his name, standing on the sea of glass, having harps of God.

I saw something like a sea of glass mingled with fire. In the Old Testament Temple of Solomon, there was a laver where the priest washed his hands before he entered into the presence of God. It was sometimes called a "sea" (I Kings 7:23). In chapter four when the apostle John looked at the laver in Heaven, he noticed that there was no water in it, it was glass. In Heaven, there will be no need for continual cleansing. We are made clean once and for all through the blood of Jesus Christ (I John 1:9). Here, the "sea" is mingled with "fire," and is occupied by those Tribulation saints that have refused to become a part of the Antichrist's kingdom. They have come through "fiery trials," and now stand on the "sea of glass" before the Throne of God in Heaven.

Over the beast. The "beast" is the Antichrist (Revelation 13:1-10).

Over his image. The "image" is a statue of the Antichrist that will be given "life" by the False Prophet (Revelation 13:1415).

Over his mark. The "mark" will be placed on all those who are a part of the Antichrist's kingdom and will enable them to buy and sell (Revelation13:16-17).

Over the number of his name. The number of the Antichrist is "666," and signifies "man attempting to be God" (Revelation 13:18).

Having the harps of God. These Tribulation saints, are given "harps," the instrument of praise. They join the other saints in their praise to God.

VERSE 3

They sing the song of Moses, the servant of God, and the song of the Lamb, saying: "Great and marvelous are Your works, Lord God Almighty! Just and true are Your ways, 0 King of the saints!

They sing the song of Moses ... and of the Lamb. Only those who have been redeemed can join in the singing of this "new song," for this is a song sung from the heart of one who has experienced the marvelous grace and mighty deliverance of Almighty God. This "new song" contains two stanzas. The first is the Song of Moses, which was a song of deliverance from earthly enemies (Exodus 15). The second stanza is the Song of the Lamb, which is a song of salvation through the Grace of God.

Great and marvelous are Your works. The word "great" is megas and means "mighty." "Marvelous" is thauma and means "to gaze at with wonder." The saints praise God for His works that are "mighty" and "awe inspiring," or almost beyond belief.

Lord God Almighty. The phrase literally reads "0 Lord God the Almighty." "Lord" is kurios, and was used by the Jews to refer to the "reigning monarch." "God" is theos, and means "the one true God." Theos with few exceptions, is the translation of the Hebrew words Elohim, which refers to God's power and preeminence, and "Jehovah" which refers to God's immutable, eternal, self-sustained existence. "Almighty" is the word pantokrator and means "ruler of all." These Tribulation saints praise God for His mighty works, and also for His nature. He is the King of all, the eternal, never-changing God.

Just and true are Your ways. The word "just" is dikaios, and means "righteous." The word "true is alethinos and means "true in the sense of being genuine." The saints praise God that His works are not only mighty, but they are right and real. Whatever God does is right, even though we may not understand it (Romans 11:33).

0 King of the saints. Some manuscripts have "King of the Nations." Either way the message is true, for "every knee shall bow" (Romans 14:11 and Philippians 2:10).

VERSE 4
Who shall not fear You, 0 Lord, and glorify Your name? For You alone are holy. For all nations shall come and worship before You, For Your judgments have been manifested."

Who shall not fear You, 0 Lord. Since the above is true, who in their right mind would not "fear" God and give "glory" to Him? The word "fear" is pobos, and means to have "a reverential fear of displeasing God." The Bible says "The fool has said in his heart, there is no God" (Psalms 14:1 and 53:1).

And glorify Your name. The word "glorify" is doxazo and means "to give honor to someone because in your estimation they are worthy."

For You alone are holy. The word "holy" is hagios, and means "that which is separate or different." There is no other being like God. He is unique!

For all nations shall come and worship before You. One day all nations of the world will pay homage unto the true God (Isaiah 45:23 and Romans 14:1).

For Your judgments have been manifested. The word "judgments" is krisis, and means "decisions." The phrase "are made manifest" (KJV) is literally "have been manifested." The word "manifest" is emphanes, and means "to shine forth, or to reveal." One day the decisions that God made regarding our lives, the course of history, etc., will be made plain to us. We will understand in full God's ways (I Corinthians 13:9-12).

VERSE 5
After these things I looked, and behold, the temple of the tabernacle of the testimony in heaven was opened.

After these things I looked. After John sees the wonder of the seven angels with the seven plagues, he looks to see what is next.

The temple of the tabernacle of the testimony in heaven. The word "temple" is naos, and refers not to the Temple as a whole, but that part of the Temple known as the "Holy Of Holies." "The Holy of Holies" was commonly called the "tabernacle of the testimony" (Exodus 38:21; Numbers 1:50, 53; 9:15; and 10:11) because it was a visible testimony to God's mercy even though man had sinned. The Holy of Holies contained three things:

1. The second table of stone which reminded the people of their rejection of the Law of God (Deuteronomy 10:1-5)

2. The manna which reminded the people of their rejection of God's daily provisions (Exodus 16:33-34)

3. Aaron's rod that budded which reminded the people of their rejection of God's leadership (Numbers 17:10)

These three things were a constant reminder to the people of their sin, and the basis upon which God's judgment was dispensed. That is why this picture is mentioned here. The seven angels are about to dispense God's judgments, and the Holy of Holies is opened to show why judgment is coming.

VERSE 6

And out of the temple came the seven angels having the seven plagues, clothed in pure bright linen, and having their chests girded with golden bands.

Out of the temple came the seven angels. The seven angels with the seven vials of judgment come from the Temple, or the very presence of God. Hence, God is the source of the judgments that are about to take place on earth.

Clothed in pure bright linen. This is the typical garment of the inhabitants of Heaven (Revelation 4:4). They represent purity and holiness. These angels are holy angels of the Almighty God.

And having their chests girded with golden bands. "Gold" symbolizes purity. The "girdle" (KJV) symbolizes service. Jesus put on a girdle (apron), and washed the disciple's feet (John 13:1-4). These angels are the holy servants of God about to dispense judgment upon the earth.

VERSE 7

Then one of the four living creatures gave to the seven angels seven golden bowls full of the wrath of God who lives forever and ever.

One of the four living creatures gave to the seven angels. The four beasts (KJV) are described in Revelation 4:6. The word "beast" is zoa which mean "living creatures." Ezekiel tells us that these creatures are angelic beings called "cherubim" (Ezekiel 10:20), and it is their responsibility to guard the holiness of God (Ezekiel 1:22-28). Isaiah refers to them as "seraphim" (Isaiah 6:2).

Seven golden bowls full. The word "vial" (KJV) is phiale, and means "a shallow bowl used for pouring libations" (I Chronicles 52:18; Zechariah 9:15; and 14:20). These bowls are not full of incense as in Revelation 5:8, but, the wrath of God. The word "full" is gemo and was used "to describe a ship that was heavily laden, almost to the point of sinking." These bowls are heavy laden with God's final judgments.

Who lives forever and ever. This is the strongest Greek phrase to describe eternity. It literally means "unto the age of the ages."

VERSE 8
The temple was filled with smoke from the glory of God and from His power, and no one was able to enter the temple till the seven plagues of the seven angels were completed.

The temple was filled with smoke from the glory of God. The word "filled" is literally "filled to capacity." "Smoke" is often used as a visible sign of God's presence and glory (Exodus 19:18, and Isaiah 6:5).

No one was able to enter the temple. The final judgments of God are so awesome that no one is allowed into His presence until they are concluded. There is no time now for intercession!

REVELATION 16

VERSE BY VERSE

THE SEVEN VIALS

THE FIRST VIAL (16:1-2)

VERSE 1

Then I heard a loud voice from the temple saying to the seven angels, "Go and pour out the bowls of the wrath of God on the earth."

I heard a loud voice from the temple. This mighty voice is not that of an angel as in 5:2, 7:2, 10:3, 14:7, etc., but of God Himself, since Revelation 15:8 said that no one could enter the Temple until the seven plagues were fulfilled.

Pour out the bowls. God commands the seven angels to begin pouring out the judgments upon earth. The seven vials (10V) represent God's final judgments on earth. There is no further hesitation and the emptying of the bowls occurs very rapidly.

VERSE 2

So the first went and poured out his bowl upon the earth, and a foul and loathsome sore came upon the men who had the mark of the beast and those who worshiped his image.

The first went and poured out is bowl. The first angel immediately obeys God's command.

A foul [noisome] and loathsome [grievous] sore. The word "noisome" is kakos, and means "evil or bad." The word "grievous" is poeros and means "painful." The word "sore is helkos and means a "malignant sore that is incurable." When the first angel pours out his bowl, and evil, painful cancer similar to that of the Egyptian plagues (Exodus 9:9-11), will come upon men.

Upon the men who had the mark of the beast and those who worshiped his image. As with the Egyptian plagues, they come only upon those who are the enemies of God.

THE SECOND VIAL (16:3)

VERSE 3

Then the second angel poured out his bowl on the sea, and it became blood as of a dead man; and every living creature in the sea died.

Poured out his bowl on the sea. The second bowl is poured out and the sea becomes like the blood of a dead man, coagulated and rotting. This is similar to the second Trumpet judgment in Revelation 8:8 and the first Egyptian plague

(Exodus 7:20, 21). The picture here is that of a man who has been murdered, and is weltering in his blood.

Every living creature in the sea died. The difference between the second trumpet and the second bowl is that here everything in the sea dies not just one third of the creatures.

THE THIRD VIAL (16:4-7)

VERSE 4

Then the third angel poured out his bowl on the rivers and springs of water, and they became blood.

Poured out his bowl on the rivers and springs. The angel pours out his judgment upon the fresh waters. This judgment is similar to the third trumpet judgment (Revelation 8:10, 11).

They became blood. The fresh waters are turned into blood; hence there is no fresh water to drink. God's judgment in these concluding hours is indeed harsh.

VERSE 5

And I heard the angel of the waters saying: "You are righteous, 0 Lord, The One who is and who was and who is to be, Because You have judged these things.

I heard the angel of the waters saying. The Jews believed that every natural element had an angel over it. In Revelation 7:1, there were four angels in control of the winds. In Revelation 14:18 and angel had power over the fire. Here, the angel over the waters speaks.

You are righteous, 0 Lord. The angel says that God is right in turning the fountains of fresh water into blood.

The One who is and who was and who is to be. This is a reference to the name "Jehovah "which means the "eternal God." The source of this judgment is the eternal God.

Because You have judged these things. God is right in doing what He has done.

VERSE 6
For they have shed the blood of saints and prophets, And You have given them blood to drink. For it is their just due."

For they have shed the blood of saints and prophets. "They" refers to those who are a part of the Antichrist's kingdom. These wicked men have slain God's righteous servants.

And you have given them blood to drink. This is the unchanging Law of Retribution. Throughout the Tribulation Period, the forces of Satan have spilled the blood of the saints as if it were no more than water. Now, because of these acts of infamy, they are getting their fill of blood. These bloodthirsty individuals are getting just what they deserve.

For it is their just due. This does not refer to moral quality, but that they deserve the judgment that is coming.

VERSE 7

And I heard another from the altar saying, "Even so, Lord God Almighty, true and righteous are Your judgments."

And I heard another from the altar. A second witness affirms the righteous judgments of God.

THE FOURTH VIAL (16:8-9)

VERSE 8

Then the fourth angel poured out his bowl on the sun, and power was given to him to scorch men with fire.

The fourth angel poured out his bowl on the sun. The fourth judgment is upon the sun.

Power was given to him to scorch men with fire. The fourth trumpet judgment only affected one third of the sun, but here the judgment is complete. The sun's rays will be intensified and as a result men will be scorched by their heat. The word "scorch" is kaumotizo and means "to burn."

VERSE 9

And men were scorched with great heat, and they blasphemed the name of God who has power over these plagues; and they did not repent and give Him glory.

And men were scorched with great heat. In recent years we have experienced "heat-waves," but nothing like what will occur during the Tribulation Period.

They blasphemed the name of God. To "blaspheme" means "to speak evil against." The "name" of God refers to the "character of God." These evil men will blaspheme God's character because of the plagues which He will send.

They did not repent and give Him glory. in spite of all the suffering these people are experiencing, they still refuse to repent and turn to God. Like Pharoah, their hearts have become hardened (Exodus 7:13, 22; and 8:15, 19, 32-35).

THE FIFTH VIAL (16:10-11)

VERSE 10

Then the fifth angel poured out his bowl on the throne of the beast, and his kingdom became full of darkness; and they gnawed their tongues because of the pain.

The fifth angel poured out his bowl on the throne of the beast. The word "seat" (KJV) is thronos, and means "throne." The "Beast is the Antichrist.

His kingdom became full of darkness. Since the Antichrist's kingdom will be worldwide, the judgment will also cover the earth. It will be pitch black, so dark you can feel it. This is similar to the Egyptian plague (Exodus 10:22) and the fourth trumpet (Revelation 8:12).

They gnawed their tongues because of the pain. The anguish of the first five vials of God's wrath will be so great that they will chew their tongues in pain.

VERSE 11
They blasphemed the God of heaven because of their pains and their sores, and did not repent of their deeds.

They blasphemed the God of heaven . . . and did not repent of their deeds. Again, the wicked slander God, and refuse to repent.

THE SIXTH VIAL (16:12-16)

VERSE 12

Then the sixth angel poured out his bowl on the great river Euphrates, and its water was dried up, so that the way of the kings from the east might be prepared.

The sixth angel poured out his bowl on the great river Euphrates. The sixth judgment is against the Euphrates River, the ancient boundary between Israel and her enemies (Genesis 15:18).

And its water was dried up. Just as God dried up the Jordan River for His people, so shall He dry up the Euphrates to allow the nations of the Far East to gather for the great Battle of Armageddon. The Euphrates flows some eighteen hundred miles from the mountains to the Persian Gulf. It is too deep to ford, and too long to go around. For centuries, it served as a protective boundary for Israel, but with the sixth vial, it dries up, and makes it easy for the enemy to enter into Israel.

The kings from the east. Perhaps this is a reference to China, India, or some other nation in the Orient.

VERSE 13

And I saw three unclean spirits like frogs coming out of the mouth of the dragon, out of the mouth of the beast, and out of the mouth of the false prophet.

I saw three unclean spirits like frogs. These "unclean spirits" are not "frogs," but "like frogs." The plagues of Egypt, where the frogs covered the land, are no doubt in John's mind. The frog was considered to be an unclean animal (Leviticus 11:10).

Coming out of the mouth of the dragon, the beast, and false prophet. The three unclean demon spirits proceed from Satan, the Antichrist, and the False Prophet.

VERSE 14

For they are spirits of demons, performing signs, which go out to the kings of the earth and of the whole world, to gather them to the battle of that great day of God Almighty.

For they are spirits of demons. This phrase literally reads "they are demon spirits." This, again, identifies their nature. They are vile demonic beings sent out by the Satanic Trinity.

Performing signs. They will be empowered by Satan to work mighty miracles, in order to deceive the world (II Thessalonians 2:9).

Which go out to the kings of the earth. Their goal is to unite the whole world under the rule of the Antichrist so that they can fight against God in the Battle of Armageddon.

To the battle of that great day of God Almighty. This is a reference to the Battle of Armageddon. This will be the battle to end all battles.

VERSE 15

"Behold, I am coming as a thief. Blessed is he who watches, and keeps his garments, lest he walk naked and they see his shame."

Behold, I am coming as a thief. The voice of Christ breaks into the judgments (Revelation 3:3). The idea is that Jesus will come to judge the wicked at the Battle of Armageddon, and the enemy will not be expecting Him, and therefore be unprepared.

Blessed is he who watches, and keeps his garments. This is the third of seven beatitudes in the book of Revelation. The wicked will be caught by surprise, but those who are watching, and serving Jesus, will be blessed when He comes.

Lest he walk naked and they see his shame. The wicked will be exposed for all to see (Luke 12:2, 3).

VERSE 16

And they gathered them together to the place called in Hebrew, Armageddon.

And they gathered them together to the place called Armageddon. "He" should be "they," and refers to the unclean spirits. Armageddon has played an important part in the history of Israel. It is estimated that over two hundred major battles have been fought in the area. The two most famous were: (1) Barak over the Canaanites (Judges 4:15); and (2) Gideon over the Midianites (Judges 7). Two great disasters also occurred at Armageddon: (1) The death of King Saul (I Samuel 31:8) and (2) The death of Josiah (II Kings 23:29, 30; and II Chronicles 35:22). Napoleon, upon visiting Armageddon, described it as the most perfect place on earth for a war.

THE SEVENTH VIAL (16:17-21)

VERSE 17

Then the seventh angel poured out his bowl into the air, and a loud voice came out of the temple of heaven, from the throne, saying, "It is done!"

The seventh angel poured out his bowl into the air. This judgment is upon the air, and will affect every living soul.

A loud voice came out of the temple of heaven from the throne, saying. Again, the voice heard is not that of an angel but that of Almighty God.

It is done. The phrase is tetelestat and means "to bring to its desired end." The last time that God spoke these words was when Jesus hung upon the cross, just before His death. At that moment, God's plan for man's salvation had come to the desired end. Now, at the end of the Tribulation Period, once again, God speaks tetelestai. It has ended just as God foreordained that it would!

Hallelujah!

VERSE 18

And there were noises and thunderings and lightnings; and there was a great earthquake, such a mighty and great earthquake as had not occurred since men were on the earth.

There were noises and thunderings and lightnings. When God Almighty finally says "It is finished," the resulting climax is "shouts, and lightning and thunder." And there was a great earthquake. Another result is a mighty earthquake, such as has never occurred on the earth before.

VERSE 19

Now the great city was divided into three parts, and the cities of the nations fell. And great Babylon was remembered before God, to give her the cup of the wine of the fierceness of His wrath.

The great city was divided into three parts. "The great city" is "Babylon, the capital of the Antichrist" (Revelation 11:18, 14:8, 17:18, and 18:2, 10, 16). It is divided into three parts by the earthquake.

The cities of the nations fell. The earthquake will be so great that it will destroy all the cities of the world.

And great Babylon was remembered before God. The phrase is literally "God remembered Great Babylon. " The Bible teaches that every deed of the wicked is stored up. God doesn't forget! Babylon's wickedness is now being rewarded.

To give her the cup of the wine of the fierceness of His wrath. This reminds us of Revelation 14:10. In Bible days, a king would take a cup of poison, and hand it to a condemned prisoner to drink as a means of execution. This is the picture here. God is going to give those who become a part of the Antichrist's system a cup to drink. it will not be filled with poison, but rather the white-hot wrath of Almighty God.

VERSE 20

Then every island fled away, and the mountains were not found.

Then every island fled away. The islands will sink into the sea.

The mountains were not found. The mountains will disappear.

VERSE 21

And great hail from heaven fell upon men, each hailstone about the weight of a talent. Men blasphemed God because of the plague of the hail, since that plague was exceedingly great.

And great hail from heaven fell upon men. In the Bible, hail is often used as an instrument of God's judgment (Exodus 9:24; Joshua 10:11; Isaiah 28:12; and Ezekiel 38:22).

Each hailstone about the weight of a talent. A "talent" weighed about one hundred pounds. The world has never known such a catastrophe. In Leviticus 24:16, God commanded that "blasphemers" be stoned to death. This may be God's way of stoning end-time blasphemers.

Men blasphemed God because of the plague of hail. Even in their death, they blaspheme God!

REVELATION 17

THE SEVEN DOOMS

INTRODUCTION

In chapter sixteen, the seven vials of judgment were poured out upon the earth. With the pouring out of the seventh vial, the judgments of God are concluded. Beginning in chapter seventeen, the apostle John adds more detail to these final judgments of the enemies of God.

This section is often referred to as the "Seven Dooms." They are as follows:

1. The Doom of "Religious Babylon" (17:1-18:24)

2. The Doom of "Commercial Babylon" (18:1-24)

3. The Doom of the Beast (19:20)

4. The Doom of the False Prophet (19:20)

5. The Doom of the Nations (19:21)

6. The Doom of Satan (20:10)

7. The doom of the Wicked (20:11-15)

In chapters seventeen and eighteen, we see the first doom. It is the destruction of the Antichrist's world system, referred to as Babylon. In chapter seventeen, we see the destruction of his religious system, and then in chapter eighteen, his commercial and political system. The Antichrist's religion will be so close to the truth that millions of people will be deceived by it. There will be a great ecumenical church and its political counterpart which the Antichrist will use to rule the world during the Tribulation Period.

THE DOOM OF RELIGIOUS BABYLON (17:1-18)

VERSE 1

Then one of the seven angels who had the seven bowls came and talked with me, saying to me, "Come, I will show you the judgment of the great harlot who sits on many waters,

Then one of the seven angels who had the seven bowls. It is fitting that one of the seven angels that had the seven bowls of God's final judgment should explain to John the judgment of Babylon.

I will show you the judgment of the great harlot. The word "whore" (10V) is krimo, and refers to the false religious system of the Antichrist during the Tribulation Period—"Religious Babylon." In Revelation 14:8, Babylon is identified as a harlot that had seduced the nations. Further evidence as to the identity of the "harlot" is found in verse five of this chapter. In contrast, the true church of Jesus Christ is referred to as a "chaste bride."

Who sits on many waters. This phrase is explained in verse fifteen, and refers to "peoples and multitudes, and nations, and tongues." This religious system will encompass the world.

VERSE 2

"with whom the kings of the earth committed fornication, and the inhabitants of the earth were made drunk with the wine of her fornication."

The kings of the earth committed fornication. This refers to "spiritual" fornication. The rulers of the world have become a part of her wicked idolatrous religious system.

Were made drunk with the wine of her fornication. "Were made drunk" means "they are under the control of." They are under her control because they are drinking her fornication (Romans 6:16).

VERSE 3

So he carried me away in the Spirit into the wilderness. And I saw a woman sitting on a scarlet beast which was full of names of blasphemy, having seven heads and ten horns.

So he carried me away in the Spirit into the wilderness. The angel carries John away in the spirit to a "desert place."

I saw a woman sitting on a scarlet beast. The woman mentioned here is the "great whore" referred to in verse one. Here, the "whore" is seen sitting upon the "Beast." This false religion will ride the Beast to power. The Beast has already been identified in chapter thirteen as the Antichrist. Here, the Beast is said to be "scarlet colored," or covered with blood as a result of his bloody reign.

VERSE 4

The woman was arrayed in purple and scarlet, and adorned with gold and precious stones and pearls, having in her hand a golden cup full of abominations and the filthiness of her fornication.

The woman was arrayed in purple and scarlet. In Bible days purple and scarlet were the colors of wealth and royalty. We have already seen in verse two of this chapter that the kings of the earth will be a part of this religious system.

Adorned with gold and precious stones and pearls. This false church will be very wealthy.

In her hand a golden cup. This description is probably taken from Jeremiah 51:7. The contents of this cup are used to bring the nations of the world under her control (Revelation 14:8).

Full of abominations and the filthiness of her fornication. What will this false church use to entice the nations of the world? The contents are identified. The cup is full of "abominations." This is the word bdelugma and refers to "something that appears acceptable, but is totally disgusting to God." The things that this false church do appear to be right, but they are disgusting to God (Proverbs 14:12). The cup is also full of "filthiness." This is the word perkiatharma, and means "the refuse that is thrown away after cleaning." It refers to that which is totally worthless and despicable.

VERSE 5

And on her forehead a name was written: MYSTERY, BABYLON THE GREAT, THE MOTHER OF HARLOTS AND OF THE ABOMINATIONS OF THE EARTH.

And on her forehead a name was written. In Rome, during ancient times, harlots wore headbands on their brows with their names on them. This identified them as harlots.

VERSE 6

I saw the woman, drunk with the blood of the saints and with the blood of the martyrs of Jesus. And when I saw her, I marveled with great amazement.

I saw the woman, drunk with the blood of the saints. This false religious system will be responsible for murdering multitudes of the saints of God during the Tribulation Period (Revelation 6:9 and 16:6).

I marveled with great amazement. The church of John's day was poor, hated by the rulers of the world, and faithfully serving Jesus. When John saw this false church of the Tribulation Period, he was amazed, and wondered with great "wonder" (KM) (thauma). This church was rich, supported by the rulers of the world, and killing the servants of God. It is no wonder that he was astonished at what he saw.

VERSE 7

But the angel said to me, "Why did you marvel? I will tell you the mystery of the woman and of the beast that carries her, which has the seven heads and the ten horns.

I will tell you the mystery of the woman. The angel, seeing John's astonishment, explains what he has just seen.

VERSE 8

"The beast that you saw was, and is not, and will ascend out of the bottomless pit and go to perdition. And those who dwell on the earth will marvel, whose names are not written in the Book of Life from the foundation of the world, when they see the beast that was, and is not, and yet is.

The beast that you saw. The "Beast" is the Antichrist (Revelation 13:1-10).

Was, and is not, and will ascend out of the bottomless pit. The phrase "was and is not" no doubt refers to the fake death and resurrection of the Antichrist in Revelation 13:1-10. The phrase "will ascend out of the bottomless pit" refers to Revelation 11:7, where we are told that the "Beast" ascended from the bottomless pit.

And go to perdition. The word "perdition" is appollumi, and means "to utterly destroy." The idea is not extinction, but "ruin." This refers to Revelation 19:20 where the "Beast" will be thrown into the "Lake of Fire."

Those who dwell on the earth will marvel (wonder, KM). It will be amazing to them that one who had so much power, and such great empire could ever fall.

Whose names are not written in the book of life. Only the wicked will be amazed. It comes as no surprise to the saints of God. We have "read the last chapter." We know that in the end, Satan shall be defeated, and our God shall reign. The phrase "Book of Life" is derived from the ancient custom of keeping genealogical records, and enrolling citizens for various purposes (Nehemiah 7:5- 64; 12:22 & 23; Jeremiah 22:30; and Ezekiel 13:9). In the Bible God is represented as having a record in the "Book of Life" of all who are His. To be blotted out of the "Book of Life" is to be cut off from God's favor. The Book of Life is the record of the righteous who are to inherit eternal life (Philippians 4:3; Revelation 3:5; 13:8 & 17:8 and 21:27).

From the foundation of the world. The Bible teaches that God, in His omniscience, wrote the names of His own in His book, before the world was created (Romans 8:29-30 and Ephesians 1:4-5).

Was, and is not, and yet is. This again, is a reference to the fake resurrection of the Antichrist (Revelation 13:1-10).

VERSE 9

"Here is the mind which has wisdom: The seven heads are seven mountains on which the woman sits.

Here is the mind which has wisdom. This is the same idea that we found in Revelation 13:18. The meaning here is that a person who is wise will heed what is about to be said.

The seven heads are seven mountains on which the woman sits. The Bible is always its own best commentary. Here, the vision of John concerning religious Babylon is about to be interpreted. The "woman" is the "harlot" already identified as "Babylon" because of her wicked character. She sits upon "seven mountains," which many believe refers to the "Seven Hills of Rome." The city of Rome, during John's day was referred to as the "City of Seven Hills." These hills were named Palatine, Aventine, Caelian, Esquiline, Vimihal, Quirinal, and Capitoline. If the seat of the Antichrist's religious kingdom is Rome, then some have concluded that the Roman Catholic Church will be the false church of the Antichrist during the Tribulation Period.

VERSE 10

"There are also seven kings. Five have fallen, one is, and the other has not yet come. And when he comes, he must continue a short time.

There are also seven kings. There are seven kings that will rule over the Seven Hills of Rome, or the Roman Empire.

Five have fallen, one is, and the other has not yet come. At the time of John's writing, there had been five great kings that had ruled over the Roman Empire: Caesar Augustus, Claudius, Caligula, Tiberius, and Nero. These "are fallen." "One is" refers to the current ruler, Domitian. "One is yet to come" refers to the Antichrist that will rule the world from a revived Roman Empire during the Tribulation Period.

And when he comes, he must continue a short time. His kingdom will last a short time, only seven years during the Tribulation Period.

VERSE 11

"And the beast that was, and is not, is himself also the eighth, and is of the seven, and is going to perdition.

And the beast that was, and is not, is himself also the eighth. The "beast" (Antichrist) is referred to as the seventh and also the eighth, probably because of his staged death and resurrection (Revelation 13:1-10). It may also refer to the fact that the Antichrist begins his reign on a platform of peace. He comes as the deliverer of the world, but midway through the Tribulation Period, he changes and becomes a different person. He becomes a great enemy of the people of God, especially the nation of Israel. His personality is so split, that John says he is not only the seventh, but also the eighth.

And is going to perdition. Again, as in verse eight, we are given the destiny of the Beast. "Perdition" is apollumi, and is the word used to describe the eternal destiny of the wicked.

VERSE 12

"The ten horns which you saw are ten kings who have received no kingdom as yet, but they receive authority for one hour as kings with the beast.

The ten horns which you saw are ten kings. The ten horns of the Beast are ten kings, or the rulers of the Kingdoms (Daniel 7:23-24). These nations will form the nucleus of the Beast's commercial and political power.

Who have received no kingdom as yet, but receive authority for one hour as kings with the beast. The Antichrist will cause their rise to power. Their kingdom will be brief, only "one hour." The phrase is mian horan, and is not to be taken literally, but to refer to a brief period of time. Since they derive their power from the Antichrist, their reign will be brief, just like his. (Revelation 17:10).

VERSE 13

"These are of one mind, and they will give their power and authority to the beast.

These are of one mind. The word "mind" is gnome and means "purpose." These are united in their goal to rule the world.

They will give their power and authority to the beast. They align themselves with the Antichrist. Indeed they do, for they shall form the base from which he will rule the world.

VERSE 14

"These will make war with the Lamb, and the Lamb will overcome them, for He is Lord of lords and King of kings; and those who are with Him are called, chosen, and faithful."

These will make war with the Lamb. This federation of nations will make war against the "Lamb," The Lord Jesus Christ (John 1:29 and Revelation 5:6).

The Lamb will overcome them. There is no doubt as to who will be the victor.

For He is Lord of lords and King of kings. The Lamb has been given supreme power (Matthew 28:18), therefore, all kings and princes must ultimately come under His rule.

Those who are with Him are called, chosen, and faithful. The phrase "those who are with Him" literally, reads "they shall also overcome that are with Him." If we suffer for Him, we will also reign with Him (II Timothy 2:12). Usually the terms "called" and "chosen" refer to the same idea. However, in the parable of the wedding garment (Matthew 22:14), they are different. Those "called" refers to those who are invited. Those "chosen" refers to those who accepted the invitation, or the "elect." The word "elect" usually refers to those who have been "called" and have "accepted." Those who are "called" and "chosen" are the "elect of God" and they will be "faithful" (Matthew 10:22).

VERSE 15

Then he said to me, "The waters which you saw, where the harlot sits, are peoples, multitudes, nations, and tongues.

And he said to me. The angel with the vial continues the explanation of what John has seen.

The waters which you saw...are peoples. This refers to the worldwide influence this false religious system will have.

VERSE 16

"And the ten horns which you saw on the beast, these will hate the harlot, make her desolate and naked, eat her flesh and burn her with fire.

The ten horns which you saw on the beast. The ten horns here represent the ten nations which will serve as the political and commercial base from which the Antichrist will rule the world (Revelation 17:12).

These will hate the harlot. The Antichrist will use his false religious system to help in his conquest of the world. However, when religious Babylon is of no further benefit to him, he and the ten nations, which serve as his commercial and political base, will turn against it.

And make her desolate. They shall strip her of all of her power. And naked. They will strip her of her adornments (Revelation 17:4). Eat her flesh. This phrase means that they shall take her wealth.

And burn her with fire. "Fire" was a symbol of utter destruction. This false religious system will be utterly destroyed by the Antichrist and his political confedcration of nations.

VERSE 17

"For God has put it into their hearts to fulfill His purpose, to be of one mind, and to give their kingdom to the beast, until the words of God are fulfilled.

For God has put it into their hearts to fulfill His purpose. God is never pleased with systems of worship which do not give Him His rightful place. Thus, "Religious Babylon," this false church, will be destroyed. God can even use the wicked to accomplish His purposes (Judges 3:8; 12 and 4:1-2).

And give their kingdom to the beast. The power and wealth that this false religion will enjoy for a brief season, will be assumed by the Antichrist.

VERSE 18

"And the woman whom you saw is that great city which reigns over the kings of the earth."

And the woman whom you saw. The "woman" is the "great whore." This is a reference to the false religious system of the Antichrist—Religious Babylon.

That great city which reigns over the kings of the earth. The false church is referred to as the great city of "Babylon" because it is so wicked. The physical location of this church will probably be Rome (Revelation 17:9).

REVELATION 18

VERSE BY VERSE

SEVEN DOOMS—continued

INTRODUCTION

In chapter seventeen, we saw the destruction of "Religious Babylon." In this chapter, we see the destruction of "Commercial and Political Babylon." These two events appear to be separate and distinct as seen by the following facts:

1. The announcement in chapter seventeen is made by one of the seven "vial angels" (17:1). The announcement here is made by "another angel" (18:1).

2. The statement "after these things" (18:1), literally means "after the events previously described," or the destruction of "Religious Babylon.

3. In chapter seventeen, verse sixteen, Babylon was utterly destroyed, and therefore it would be impossible for the same kingdom to be destroyed again in chapter eighteen.

THE DOOM OF COMMERCIAL BABYLON (18:1-24)

VERSE 1

After these things I saw another angel coming down from heaven, having great authority, and the earth was illuminated with his glory.

After these things I saw another angel. After the destruction of "Religious Babylon," John saw another angel come from Heaven.

And the earth was illuminated with his glory. As always, this is only "reflected" glory. The angel is reflecting the glory of God from whose presence he has come.

VERSE 2

And he cried mightily with a loud voice, saying, "Babylon the great is fallen, is fallen, and has become a dwelling place of demons, a prison for every foul spirit, and a cage for every unclean and hated bird!

And he cried mightily with a loud voice. The angel cried out with a loud voice, so that all could hear, and none could misunderstand.

Babylon the great is fallen is fallen. In the Greek, it is past tense, and literally reads "Babylon the great did fall." How can this be past tense if it has not yet occurred? Many times in scripture, God pronounces things which are not as of yet a reality, as though they were. In Isaiah 53, God speaks of the cross as though it were already an accomplished fact, when in reality this passage was written over six hundred years before the birth of Jesus. Since God is omnipotent, whatever He wills to do, He can accomplish. It is as sure as though it were already a reality.

And has become a dwelling place of demons (devils-KJV). This phrase literally means "has become he dwelling place of demons." This describes the vileness of the Antichrist's political system. The Antichrist will be energized by the Devil, and will be aided by demons loosed from the bottomless pit (Revelation 9).

A prison for every foul spirit. The word "hold" is phulake, and means "a watchtower or stronghold." The idea here is that the demons are dwelling in the city and keeping a watch over it, or guarding it.

A cage for every unclean and hated bird. The word "cage" is also phulake, and means "watchtower or stronghold." The word "unclean" is akathartos and means "impure or that which is totally opposite to God." The word "hateful" is miseo and, here, should read "hated." The word "bird" is orneou and is sometimes used to refer to the "vulture." "Babylon" has become the dwelling place of demons and the stronghold of all that is impure. Those who prey on others like vultures congregate here.

VERSE 3

"For all the nations have drunk of the wine of the wrath of her fornication, the kings of the earth have committed fornication with her, and the merchants of the earth have become rich through the abundance of her luxury."

For all nations have drunk of ... her fornication. The vile and wicked of all nations have congregated here.

The kings of earth have committed fornication. The world rulers have become a part of the Antichrist's political and economic system.

The merchants of the earth have become rich. Those who make their living in commerce have become a part of this vile world system. We saw in Revelation thirteen, verse seventeen, that the only way a person will be able to buy or sell during the Tribulation Period will be to become a part of the Antichrist's system and receive his mark.

Through the abundance of her luxury. The kingdom of the Antichrist will be very wealthy, and those who become a part of it will reap the benefits.

VERSE 4

And I heard another voice from heaven saying, "Come out of her, my people, lest you share in her sins, and lest you receive of her plagues.

I heard another voice from heaven saying. Another angel cries out to those saints of God on earth who are not a part of the Antichrist's system.

Come out of her, my people. The command of God for these Tribulation saints is the same as it had always been for God's people (II Corinthians 6:17).

Lest you share in her sins. All of God's commands are for our benefit. The main reason God commands us to be separate from the world is in order to retain our purity. Paul said that a "little leaven, leavens the whole lump" (I Corinthians 5:6).

Lest you receive of her plagues. The second reason that we should be separate is because God must judge sin, and if we partake of the world's sins, He will have to punish us, even though we are His children (Hebrews 12:6-11).

VERSE 5

"For her sins have reached to heaven, and God has remembered her iniquities.

For her sins have reached to heaven and God has remembered. Her sins are so many that they have reached unto heaven, and God has remembered every one. It may appear at times that God forgets or ignores or sins, but He is merely storing them up. Not a one is ever forgotten until they are covered by the blood (Psalm 103:12).

VERSE 6

"Render to her just as she rendered to you, and repay her double according to her works; in the cup which she has mixed, mix double for her.

Render (reward-KJV) to her just as she rendered to you. The word "reward" is apodote and means "to render." The indictment against Babylon is so great that it calls for retribution. The angel is stating the common Old Testament law known as the lex talionis, "an eye for an eye and a tooth for a tooth" (Psalms 137:8; Jeremiah 50:15, 29; 51:24, 56 and Matthew 7:2). He is saying, render to Babylon judgment in proportion to her wickedness.

Repay her double according to her works. In certain cases, the Levitical Law required that restitution be double. The idea here is that Babylon's sins are so great that the only just recompense would be to punish her twice.

In the cup which she mixed, mix double for her. Her cup has been filled to the brim with "abominations and filthiness" (Revelation 17:4). The angel says give her twice as much judgment. God's judgment upon Babylon is harsh and severe because she has deceived and led so many others astray (Matthew 18:6, 7).

VERSE 7
"In the measure that she glorified herself and lived luxuriously, in the same measure give her torment and sorrow; for she says in her heart, 'I sit as queen, and am no widow, and will not see sorrow.'

The measure she glorified herself and lived luxuriously. This empire has been the recipient of great glory and unmatched wealth.

In the same measure give her torment and sorrow. As great as her glory and wealth was, it is nothing compared to her torment and sorrow when God's judgment comes.

For she has said in her heart. We have been given a vivid description of the outward sins of this wicked empire, now we see the inner sins of her heart. She is filled with the sin of pride. Pride was the sin that led to Satan's downfall (Isaiah 14:12-14). Pride was the sin that led to the downfall of Eve (Genesis 3:5).

I sit a queen. She prides herself in the fact that she is the bride of the Beast (Antichrist).

And am no widow. In Bible days, when a widow's husband died, except in rare occasions, she was left destitute. This shows her arrogance and self —confidence.

And will not see sorrow. Since she is the bride of the Beast, the ruler of the whole world, she thinks she will never have to "mourn." Her security in the Antichrist however, proves to be a false security. The only true security is God. All else will one day fail us.

VERSE 8

"Therefore her plagues will come in one day--death and mourning and famine. And she will be utterly burned with fire, for strong is the Lord God who judges her.

Therefore her plagues will come in one day. Since she feels secure and safe in her position as the bride of the Beast, her judgment will come unexpectedly. The phrase "one day" means "suddenly or unexpectedly."

Death and mourning and famine. These are the results of the plagues which Almighty God will pour out upon this wicked world system.

And she will be utterly burned with fire. When the Antichrist was finished with "Religious Babylon" (the false church), he utterly destroyed her with fire (Revelation 17:16). Here, God destroys his "Commercial and Political Babylon" in the same manner.

For strong is the Lord God who judges her. This harsh judgment will come to pass because it is from the Almighty God.

VERSE 9

"The kings of the earth who committed fornication and lived luxuriously with her will weep and lament for her, when they see the smoke of her burning,

The kings of the earth ... will weep and lament for her. The rulers of the whole world will weep and wail because Babylon, the source of their political and economic power, is destroyed.

VERSE 10

"standing at a distance for fear of her torment, saying, 'Alas, alas, that great city Babylon, that mighty city! For in one hour your judgment has come.'

Standing at a distance for fear of her torment. The rulers of the world stand afar off and are afraid to aid her.

Saying, alas, alas. The word "alas" is ouai and is usually translated "woe." This was the typical wail of one who had experienced extreme sorrow.

For in one hour your judgment has come. Again, the idea is that the judgment has come suddenly and unexpectedly. The kings of the earth weep and wail, almost in unbelief, that an empire as great as this could come to naught so suddenly.

VERSE 11

"And the merchants of the earth will weep and mourn over her, for no one buys their merchandise anymore:

And the merchants of the earth will weep and mourn over her. Not only do the kings lament the fall of Babylon, but also the merchants.

For no one buys their merchandise anymore. Their wail is not so much for Babylon, but for themselves.

VERSE 12

"merchandise of gold and silver, precious stones and pearls, fine linen and purple, silk and scarlet, every kind of citron wood, every kind of object of ivory, every kind of object of most precious wood, bronze, iron, and marble;

Gold and silver. In verses twelve and thirteen, their merchandise is listed. Listed here are some twenty-eight items that characterized a humanistic, materialistic, secular society during Bible days. "Gold and silver" have always been precious metals because they are rare.

Precious stones and pearls. During Bible days, precious stones were very valuable. Some even thought that precious stones had medicinal qualities. The amethyst was said to be a cure for drunkenness. The diamond was said to neutralize poison. The green jasper was said to bring fertility. The order of preference in stones among the ancients was first, diamonds; second, emeralds; third, beryls and opals; and fourth, sardonyn. The Romans loved the pearl more than any other stone.

Fine linen. Fine linen came mainly from Egypt. It was the clothing of priests and kings. It was very expensive.

Purple. Ancient purple was much redder than modern-day purple. It was the royal color and was used in the garments of the wealthy. Purple garments were extremely expensive during Bible days.

Silk. Silk, during John's day, was almost beyond price for it had to be imported from far-off China. It was so costly, that a pound of silk was sold for a pound of gold!

Scarlet. Scarlet, like purple, was a much sought after dye.

Every kind of citron wood. Citron (thyine) wood came from North Africa. It was sweet-smelling and had a beautiful grain. It was used primarily to make table tops. Since the tree from which this type of wood comes is usually small, trees large enough to provide table tops were very scarce, and extremely expensive.

Every kind of object of ivory. Ivory was used for decorative purposes such as in sculpture, statues, etc.

Every kind of object of most precious wood. This refers to furniture and other items made from expensive woods of the world.

And of bronze. Statuettes of Corinthian brass and bronze were world famous and very expensive.

And iron. Iron came from the Black Sea area and Spain.

And marble. Marble was used in expensive buildings. Augustus boasted that when he came to Rome he "found Rome of brick, but left it of marble."

VERSE 13

"and cinnamon and incense, fragrant oil and frankincense, wine and oil, fine flour and wheat, cattle and sheep, horses and chariots, and bodies and souls of men.

Cinnamon. Cinnamon emitted a sweet smell. It was a luxury item imported from India.

Incense (odors). The word is amomon. It was used as a hair dressing, and also as oil for funeral rites.

Fragrant oil. This refers to different kinds of ointments used in ceremonial rites, etc.

Frankincense. Frankincense was a resin used in worship.

Wine and oil. These were two of the three main crops of the Middle East.

Fine flour and wheat. Refers to the finest wheat flour. Barley was the bread of the poor.

Cattle and sheep, horses. This refers to livestock.

And chariots. The word here is rede, and did not refer to racing or military chariots, but rather the four-wheeled chariots of the aristocrats of Rome. They were often silver-plated.

And bodies and souls of men. This phrase is literally "bodies and even the souls of men." Human lives will become little more than merchandised (abortion, euthanasia, surrogate motherhood, etc.) during the Tribulation Period.

VERSE 14

"The fruit that your soul longed for has gone from you, and all the things which are rich and splendid have gone from you, and you shall find them no more at all.

The fruit that your soul longed for has gone from you. All of the material things that these merchants desire and worked so hard to attain will suddenly be gone (I John 2:17).

You shall find them no more at all. This phrase is a doubled double negative with future active and is the most emphatic negation possible in the Greek language. There is absolutely no possibility that they will ever have these things again.

VERSE 15
"The merchants of these things, who became rich by her, will stand at a distance for fear of her torment, weeping and wailing,

The merchants of these things ... will stand at a distance. This expresses the lament of the merchants and is a repetition of verse ten.

VERSE 16
"and saying, 'Alas, alas, that great city that was clothed in fine linen, purple, and scarlet, and adorned with gold and precious stones and pearls!

And saying, Alas, alas, that great city. These merchants will cry out in horror over the destruction of this great empire.

VERSE 17

'For in one hour such great riches came to nothing.' Every shipmaster, all who travel by ship, sailors, and as many as trade on the sea, stood at a distance

For in one hour. This does not mean a literal hour, but it means suddenly and unexpectedly.

Such great riches came to nothing. Nothing (naught) is eremoo, and means to make "totally desolate." The Antichrist will bring to naught the false system of religion centered in Rome (Religious Babylon), and God will bring to naught the world commercial system centered in Rome. But church and state powers will collapse, and nothing will be left.

Every shipmaster ... stood at a distance. First the kings stood afar off and lamented the fall of "Babylon;" then the merchants; and now the shipmasters. This refers to those who made their living shipping the merchandise. The hope of their gain is now gone with Babylon's fall.

VERSE 18

"and cried out when they saw the smoke of her burning, saying, 'What is like this great city?'

Cried out ... what is like this great city? It is hard to believe an empire this great has come to naught.

VERSE 19

"They threw dust on their heads and cried out, weeping and wailing, and saying, 'Alas, alas, that great city, in which all who had ships on the sea became rich by her wealth! For in one hour she is made desolate.'

They threw dust on their heads and cried out, weeping and wailing. This was the typical expression of grief and utter despair during Bible days (Job 2:12; Lamentations 2:10; and Ezekiel 2:30).

Became rich by her wealth. The word rich (costliness KJV) is the Greek word timios, and means "that which is precious." Ships and those who sail them will be precious or valuable during the Tribulation Period because they are needed to transport goods throughout the worldwide empire of the Antichrist.

For in one hour she is made desolate. Again, the destruction has come suddenly.

VERSE 20

"Rejoice over her, 0 heaven, and you holy apostles and prophets, for God has avenged you on her!"

Rejoice over her, 0 heaven, and you holy apostles and prophets. What causes lament on earth, causes extreme joy in heaven among the people of God (Deuteronomy 32:43; and Jeremiah 51:48).

For God has avenged you on her. In Revelation 6:10, the saints cried out to God, and asked "How long?" They were told to "Rest a while." Now, the day of vengeance has finally come!

VERSE 21

Then a mighty angel took up a stone like a great millstone and threw it into the sea, saying, "Thus with violence the great city Babylon shall be thrown down, and shall not be found anymore.

Then a mighty angel took up a stone like a great millstone. The word "millstone" is mulikos, and here refers to the large millstone which was turned by an ox or donkey to grind the grain.

And threw it into the sea. This is a symbolic gesture illustrating the total destruction of "Babylon." It is probably taken from Jeremiah 51:63-64.

Thus with violence the great city Babylon shall be thrown down. The fall of Babylon will be a violent one. This is a fitting end to an empire that has slaughtered millions during the Tribulation Period.

And shall not be found anymore. Here, again, the double negative is used; emphasizing that Babylon will never rise again.

VERSE 22

"The sound of harpists, musicians, flutists, and trumpeters shall not be heard in you anymore. No craftsman of any craft shall be found in you anymore, and the sound of a millstone shall not be heard in you anymore.

The sound of harpists, musicians, flutists, and trumpeters. In verse twenty-two, we have the death silence of a city that has been utterly destroyed. The harpers and minstrels played and sang on joyous occasions. The flute was used at festivals and the trumpet was sounded at games and official ceremonies. But, they will never be heard again. Babylon has fallen!

Shall not be heard in you anymore. Again, the double negative is used for emphasis.

No craftsman of any craft. The word "craftsman" is techne and means "those who make their living by manufacturing."

Shall be found in you anymore. The sound of manufacturing will never be heard in Babylon again.

And the sound of a millstone shall not be heard in you anymore. The grinding of grain between the millstones was a common sound, but it will be heard no more.

Revelation 18:23 NKJV 23 "The light of a lamp shall not shine in you anymore, and the voice of bridegroom and bride shall not be heard in you anymore. For your merchants were the great men of the earth, for by your sorcery all the nations were deceived.

VERSE 23

"The light of a lamp shall not shine in you anymore, and the voice of bridegroom and bride shall not be heard in you anymore. For your merchants were the great men of the earth, for by your sorcery all the nations were deceived.

If there is no life in the city, there will be no one to light a candle. The city will lie in total darkness, no sign of life whatsoever.

And the voice of bridegroom and bride. The wedding was a time of great joy and festivities. There will never again be any joyous festivities in the city of Babylon.

For you merchants were the great men of the earth. The phrase "great men" means "princes." The kings and princes of the earth were among the merchants of this great empire.

For by your sorcery all the nations were deceived. The word "sorceries" is the word pharmakeia and means "the use of medicine, drugs or spells." We get our English word "pharmacy" from it. This could be a reference to drug trafficking. However, one thing is clear; all the nations of the world were "deceived" into becoming a part of her system.

VERSE 24
"And in her was found the blood of prophets and saints, and of all who were slain on the earth."

In her was found the blood. This wicked empire was responsible for slaughtering multitudes of God's people during the Tribulation Period. Any nation which kills its prophets and saints plots its own doom (1 Chronicles 16:22 and Psalm 105:15). Joyless, dark, and silent, Babylon now stands as a monument to the vengeance of Almighty God!

REVELATION 19

BEAST, FALSE PROPHET, NATIONS

THE THREEFOLD HALLELUJAH (19:1-5)

VERSE 1

After these things I heard a loud voice of a great multitude in heaven, saying, "Alleluia! Salvation and glory and honor and power belong to the Lord our God!

After these things. The phrase is meta tauta, and has already occurred several times in the Revelation. The first five verses of chapter nineteen are actually the climax of chapters seventeen and eighteen in which Religious and Commercial Babylon were destroyed.

I heard a loud voice of a great multitude in heaven. This great host of Heaven consists of the angels, the twenty-four elders, and the four living creatures (Revelation 4:6-10; 5:8-14).

Saying, Alleluia! Salvation and glory, and honor, and power. The Heavenly host joins in a threefold hallelujah chorus of praise, after the destruction of Babylon. From this point on, the whole tenor of the book of Revelation changes, and becomes that of rejoicing, for the King is coming! The first

Hallelujah chorus is for the destruction of the great "whore" (Religious Babylon). The word "alleluia" is a transliteration of the Hebrew "hallelujah," and occurs nowhere else in the New Testament, other than the Revelation. The word was a typical expression of praise in the Old Testament (Psalms 104; 109).

It was composed of two Hebrew roots: heel, meaning "praise," and Jehovah which was the Hebrew "name for God." The meaning of the word was "Praise Jehovah, or Praise the Lord." Hence, they praise God for His judgment upon the false church of the Antichrist. "Salvation" is the word soteria, and means "deliverance." The word "glory" is doxa and means weight or worth. God is worthy of praise, and will receive it (Luke 19:40).

VERSE 2

"For true and righteous are His judgments, because He has judged the great harlot who corrupted the earth with her fornication; and He has avenged on her the blood of His servants shed by her."

For true and righteous are His judgments. Again, as the heavenly host observes what has happened on earth, they conclude that God has done what is right and just (Revelation 15:3; 16:7).

Because He has judged the great harlot (whore, KJV). The "great whore" is "Religious Babylon," the false church of the Antichrist (Revelation 17).

He has avenged on her the blood of His servants shed by her. The word "avenge" is ekdikeo, and means "justice which proceeds from justice." It is the idea of "an eye for an eye, and a tooth for a tooth." God has given to Religious Babylon that which she deserved. She destroyed the "servants of God," and now God has destroyed her.

VERSE 3

Again they said, "Alleluia! Her smoke rises up forever and ever!"

Again they said, "Alleluia! This is the second Hallelujah chorus. The host of Heaven praises God for the destruction of Commercial Babylon.

Her smoke rises up forever and ever! This refers to the destruction of Commercial Babylon (Revelation 17:9 & 18).

VERSE 4

And the twenty-four elders and the four living creatures fell down and worshiped God who sat on the throne, saying, "Amen! Alleluia!"

And the twenty-four elders. Who are the twenty-four elders? First of all, they are not angels, for the name "elder" is never applied to angels in the Bible. Neither are angels ever said to wear crowns or sit on thrones. Second, these elders are said to be sitting on thrones. They have been granted authority, and they are rulers. Third, they are clothed in white raiment, evidence that they have been redeemed by Christ's blood (Revelation 3:5, 18). Fourth, they wear crowns. The word used does not refer to the diadem, the crown of the reigning monarch. The diadem is reserved for Christ alone. The word used here is the Greek word stephanos and refers to the victor's crown, the crown awarded to those who had won an athletic event. These crowns were usually woven as a garland of oak, ivy, parsley, myrtle or olive. But, this victor's crown is made of gold (I Corinthians 9:25). Fifth, they are twenty-four in number. In the Bible, the numbers twelve and twenty-four are commonly used to designate the redeemed of God. For these reasons the twenty-four elders in Heaven seem to represent all those who have been redeemed throughout the ages. It is interesting to note that in the New Jerusalem, which is described in Revelation 21:9ff, the twelve gates of the city are named after the twelve sons of Jacob, and the twelve foundations upon which the city wall is built are named after the twelve apostles of Jesus. It appears that in the book of Revelation the twelve apostles represent the New Testament saints, and the twelve sons of Jacob represent the Old Testament saints. The two groups combined represent all the redeemed of all the ages (Mathew 19:27-29; and Revelation 5:8-10).

The four living creatures (beasts). The word "beast" is zoa which means "living creatures." Ezekiel tells us that these creatures are angelic beings called "cherubim," (Ezekiel 10:20), and it is their responsibility to guard the holiness of God (Ezekiel 1:22-28). Isaiah refers to them as "seraphim" (Isaiah 6:2).

Saying Amen; Alleluia. This is the third "Hallelujah Chorus." The word "amen" is a transliteration from Hebrew into both Greek and English. The twenty-four elders and the four creatures express their "affirmation" of God's destruction of Babylon.

VERSE 5

Then a voice came from the throne, saying, "Praise our God, all you His servants and those who fear Him, both small and great!"

Then a voice came from the throne, saying. This is not the voice of God, or the lamb. This is the voice of an "angel of the presence."

Praise our God. This phrase literally means "Give praise unto our God." The angel invites all to offer praise unto God.

Both small and great. This, again, reiterates the fact that in Heaven, there are no distinctions such as race, class, etc (I Corinthians 12:13; Galatians 3:23; and Colossians 3:11). Verse five concludes the threefold hallelujah chorus over the destruction of Babylon.

THE MARRIAGE SUPPER OF THE LAMB (19:6-10)

VERSE 6

And I heard, as it were, the voice of a great multitude, as the sound of many waters and as the sound of mighty thunderings, saying, "Alleluia! For the Lord God Omnipotent reigns!

And I heard, as it were, the voice of a great multitude. After Heavenly hosts praise God for His victory over "Babylon," they burst into praise over an event for which they have been waiting—the "marriage Supper of the Lamb."

VERSE 7

"Let us be glad and rejoice and give Him glory, for the marriage of the Lamb has come, and His wife has made herself ready."

Let us be glad and rejoice and give glory (honor) to Him. This is a time of great joy! It is a time for rejoicing, and a time to honor the "bridegroom."

For the marriage of the Lamb. In order to understand this passage, we must review the Jewish marriage custom. There were three phases to the Jewish marriage ceremony. First, there was the initial agreement where the parents arranged the marriage for the couple. This was usually done when the children were very young, and a contract was drawn up. The second phase was the actual marriage ceremony itself. This usually occurred when the children were in their teens. At this time, the bridegroom would lead a processional of friends, attended by musicians to the home of the bride (Judges 14:10; Isaiah 61:10 and Matthew 9:15). If it was night, torches were carried to the home of the bridegroom for the actual marriage ceremony. It was a time of music and dancing (Solomon 3:6-11). The third phase of the marriage was the marriage "supper" or "feast." This lasted for several days, and was a tremendous occasion. It was a time of great celebration. In the Old Testament, Israel is referred to as the bride of Jehovah (Isaiah 62:4-5; Hosea 2:19). In the New Testament, the church is referred to as the bride of Christ (Matthew 15:1; 22:2, 10, 11; Mark 2:19 and John 3:29). The apostle Paul continues this idea in his writings (II Corinthians 11:2; and Ephesians 5:21-33). The metaphor of marriage is a beautiful description of the relationship between the church and our Lord Jesus Christ. The first phase of the marriage was when God chose us (election) to be the bride of His Son (John 6:37- 40; 17:1-6; Ephesians 1:4-5; II Thessalonians 2:13; and II Timothy 1:9). The second phase will be the "Rapture" when He will come to take us to His home in Heaven.

The third phase will be the "Marriage Supper of the Lamb," described in Revelation 19:6-10.

Has (is) come. This is the prophetic aorist tense and should read "is come at last." This is the event of which the "bride" and "bridegroom" have been awaiting for centuries.

And His bride has made herself ready. In preparation for the bridegroom's coming, the bride would spend hours making herself ready. She would array herself in a white robe, jewels, and a veil (Genesis 24:65; Isaiah 61:10; and Revelation 19:8, 21:2). The church is at this present time preparing itself for the coming of her bridegroom (Ephesians 2:10 and 5:25-27)

VERSE 8

And to her it was granted to be arrayed in fine linen, clean and bright, for the fine linen is the righteous acts of the saints.

And to her it was granted. The word "granted" is didomi, and means "to give, or to bestow." This emphasizes that all that we have is a result of grace (Ephesians 2:7-9).

To be arrayed. The word "array" is peribabllo, and means "to cast around."

In fine linen, clean and bright. This is a typical expression signifying righteousness and purity (Revelation 3:4; 4:4; 6:11; 7:9, 13, 14).

The righteous acts (righteousness) of the saints. The word "righteousness" is dikaiosune, and means "righteous deeds." We are weaving in this life what we will wear in the next! Our wedding garment will be composed of our godly deeds.

VERSE 9

Then he said to me, "Write: 'Blessed are those who are called to the marriage supper of the Lamb!" And he said to me, "These are the true sayings of God."

Then he said to me. The one speaking may be one of the angels with the seven vials (Revelation 17:1).

Blessed are those who are called to the marriage supper. This is the fourth of seven beatitudes found in the book of Revelation. The word "called" is kaleo, and means those who are "bidden, or invited." This could not refer to the "church," for the church is the "bride of Christ," not an invited guest. In all probability, the "invited guests" are the Old Testament saints such as Abraham, Isaac, Jacob, etc. (Matthew 8:11, and Luke 13:28). In essence, all the righteous of all the ages and dispensations that are not included in the "bride" (the New Testament church) will be guests at the "Wedding Supper."

These are the true sayings of God. The word "true" is alethinos, and means that which is "genuine" in contrast to that which is false. What John has just heard is the "genuine" word of God. It is true, and will come to pass.

VERSE 10

And I fell at his feet to worship him. But he said to me, "See that you do not do that! I am your fellow servant, and of your brethren who have the testimony of Jesus. Worship God! For the testimony of Jesus is the spirit of prophecy."

And I fell at his feet to worship him. John is overwhelmed by what he has seen and heard from the angelic messenger, and attempts to worship him.

See that you do not do that; I am your fellow servant. The angel forbids John from worshipping him. We are all fellow-servants (Matthew 18:22ff, 24:49; Colossians 1:7, 4:7; and Revelation 6:11). No matter how great the messenger is, he is never to be the object of our worship.

Of your brethren who have the testimony of Jesus. The servants of God have been entrusted with the "testimony of Jesus," or the true witness about Jesus (Revelation 1:2, 9; 12:17; 22:4).

Worship God! The only one worthy of our worship is God Almighty (Deuteronomy 6:13, and Matthew 4:10).

For the testimony of Jesus is the spirit of prophecy. The word "spirit is pneuma, and is here used to refer to "breath." The word "prophecy" is propheted and means that which is "spoken forth." The meaning of the phrase is that the message spoken forth by the true prophet of God is always a testimony about Jesus.

THE SECOND COMING OF CHRIST (19:11-19)

VERSE 11

Now I saw heaven opened, and behold, a white horse. And He who sat on him was called Faithful and True, and in righteousness He judges and makes war.

Now I saw heaven opened. Two times in the book of Revelation, Heaven is opened. The first time was when Heaven was opened for John (the saints) to enter at the "Rapture" (Revelation 4:1). The second time is here, where Jesus returns to earth to establish His Kingdom.

A white horse ... He who sat on him was called Faithful and True. The "horse" in ancient days was the animal of war and was very powerful (Job 39). The "white horse" was the horse ridden by the king or emperor. In Revelation 6:1-2, we saw the Antichrist, riding into history upon a white horse. The rider of the "white horse" here is not the Antichrist, but the "Christ." His is the Lord Jesus, the one who is "faithful and true."

And in righteousness He judges and makes war. The first time Jesus came to earth, He was born as a babe in Bethlehem, and there was no room for Him. The second time, He will come to wage war against the "Beast," and the "False Prophet," and bring an end to the terrible years of Tribulation, at the "Battle of Armageddon." Armageddon has played an important part in the history of Israel. It is estimated that over two hundred major battles have been fought in the area. The two most famous were: [1] Barak over the Canaanites (Judges 4:15); and [2] Gideon over the Midianites (Judges 7). Two great disasters also occurred at Armageddon: [1] The death of King Saul (1 Samuel 31:8) and [2] The death of Josiah (II Kings 23:29, 30; and II Chronicles 35:22). Napoleon upon visiting Armageddon, described it as the most perfect place on earth for war. The Bible gives additional information concerning this final Battle. First, it will be fought in the Valley of Megiddo, just south of Jerusalem (Revelation 16:16). Second, the Battle of Armageddon will be preceded by an aggressive military campaign , on the part of the Antichrist, against the Jews, who will flee to the wilderness (possibly Petra) for safety (Revelation 12:6). Third, the Antichrist will assemble the greatest army ever under his coalition of ten nations (Revelation 9:16). Fourth, as these armies pass through the Valley of Megiddo, on their way to strike the final blow to the Jews, Jesus Christ will descend with His armies from Heaven (Revelation 19:11-16). Fifth, Jesus Christ will totally destroy the armies of the Antichrist (Revelation 19:21). Sixth, the destruction will be so great, that human blood will cover the entire valley at a depth of four feet (Revelation 14:20). Seventh, it will take seven years to gather and burn the broken weapons of war used by the Antichrist's armies in this battle (Ezekiel 39:9). Eighth, the vultures will be called by God to pick the carcasses clean after the battle (Revelation 19:17, 18). Ninth, it will take seven months to bury the bones of all those slain in this battle (Ezekiel 39:12).

VERSE 12

His eyes were like a flame of fire, and on His head were many crowns. He had a name written that no one knew except Himself.

His eyes were like a flame of fire. This further identifies the rider as the Lord Jesus Christ (Revelation 1:14). Jesus is coming in fiery judgment. This description is probably taken from Daniel 10:6. Fire penetrates, reveals, and burns away the dross and impurities.

On His head were many crowns. The word "crown" is diadem, and refers to the crown of the reigning monarch. In chapter one, we had a vivid description of Jesus, but the truly amazing thing was that He had no "crown." When He returns to earth in judgment (Revelation 19:11ff), He is wearing many crowns. The "crown" (diadem) that Jesus will be wearing when He returns will be made from the "crowns" (stephanos—victor's crowns) that we receive at the Judgment Seat for our faithfulness to Jesus. Our crowns will be presented to Jesus as an act of gratitude and worship (Revelation 4:10).

He had a name written that no one knew except Himself. As we have already seen on several occasions, the "name" in Bible days represented a person's character or nature. Here, the idea is that the character and nature of Jesus is beyond comprehension. The totality of the essence of God can only be known by God Himself.

VERSE 13

He was clothed with a robe dipped in blood, and His name is called The Word of God.

He was clothed with a robe dipped in blood. His cloak is covered with blood. This is not His own blood, the result of His Calvary agonies, but the blood of His enemies (Isaiah 63:3-4). This is the fulfillment of what John saw in Revelation 14:14-20.

And His name is called The Word of God. This is further identification of the rider. In John's writings he often referred to Jesus as the "Word" (John 1:1, 14). Jesus is the final and perfect revelation of God to men (Hebrews 1:1ff).

VERSE 14

And the armies in heaven, clothed in fine linen, white and clean, followed Him on white horses.

And the armies in heaven... followed Him on white horses. The armies are composed of all the righteous saints, all the hosts of Heaven. This is a fulfillment of the prophecy of Jude, "... Behold, the Lord comes with ten thousands (myriads) of His saints, to execute judgment on all..." (Jude 14).

Clothed in fine linen, white and clean. They are clothed in their wedding garments, having just left the marriage supper of the Lamb.

VERSE 15

Now out of His mouth goes a sharp sword, that with it He should strike the nations. And He Himself will rule them with a rod of iron. He Himself treads the winepress of the fierceness and wrath of Almighty God.

Now out of His mouth goes a sharp sword. The sword was the weapon of war. The sword that Jesus will use to defeat the Antichrist is not a metal one, but His spoken word (Ephesians 6:17). God "spoke' the world into existence (Genesis 1).

He should strike the nations ... And He Himself will rule them with a rod of iron. Here, the purpose of the return of Jesus is clearly given. He is coming to destroy the wicked, and to rule the world (Psalms 2:8, 9; and Isaiah 11:4).

He Himself treads the winepress of the fierceness and wrath of Almighty God. Jesus is coming to execute the judgment of His Father, the Almighty God (Revelation 14:10, 19ff; 16:19).

VERSE 16

And He has on His robe and on His thigh a name written: KING OF KINGS AND LORD OF LORDS.

And He has on His robe and on His thigh a name written: KING OF KINGS AND LORD OF LORDS. The name of the rider is clearly seen. It is written on his cloak and his thigh. There is no mistaking His identity. He is the "King of Kings, and Lord of Lords." This title is reserved for Jesus alone (I Timothy 6:15, 16; and Revelation 17:14).

VERSE 17

Then I saw an angel standing in the sun; and he cried with a loud voice, saying to all the birds that fly in the midst of heaven, "Come and gather together for the supper of the great God,

I saw an angel standing in the sun; and he cried with a loud voice. The identity of the angel is not given. His purpose, however, is clear.

Saying to all the birds that fly in the midst of heaven. The angel cries out to the "vultures" (orneois) of the air.

Come and gather together for the supper of the great God. The imagery is taken from Ezekiel 39:17. The saints of God have just finished the Marriage Supper of the Lamb, and now God ids about to prepare a supper for the vultures of the air.

VERSE 18

"that you may eat the flesh of kings, the flesh of captains, the flesh of mighty men, the flesh of horses and of those who sit on them, and the flesh of all people, free and slave, both small and great."

That you may eat the flesh. The menu for the occasion is given. It consists of the flesh of all men, and all created things. The idea is that this judgment will be upon all those who are a part of the Antichrist's kingdom.

VERSE 19

And 1 saw the beast, the kings of the earth, and their armies, gathered together to make war against Him who sat on the horse and against His army.

And I saw the beast. The beast has already been identified as the Antichrist (Revelation 13:1-10).

Gathered together to make war. This will be Satan's last effort during the Tribulation Period to defeat God. He will empower the Antichrist to gather all the nations of the world together to make war against Jesus, who has come to destroy the wicked and establish His own rule (Revelation 19:15).

THE DOOM OF THE BEAST AND FALSE PROPHET (19:20)

VERSE 20

Then the beast was captured, and with him the false prophet who worked signs in his presence, by which he deceived those who received the mark of the beast and those who worshiped his image. These two were cast alive into the lake of fire burning with brimstone.

Then the beast was captured. This is the second of the seven final dooms. The first was the doom of Babylon (Revelation 17, 18). After the Battle of Armageddon, the Antichrist will be "taken" (the Greek word is piazo, which means "to take by force") and "cast" (hallo, which also means "to hurl, or violently throw down") alive into the "Lake of Fire" which is the final place of punishment, and perpetual torment for the wicked (Revelation 20:13). It is not a place of annihilation (Revelation 20:10). The "Lake of Fire" is a place of fire and brimstone. Fire and brimstone have often been used as instruments of judgment by God (Genesis 19:24). The Beast, the False Prophet, the Devil, and all the wicked of all the ages will spend eternity in the "Lake of Fire" (Revelation 19:20; 20:10, 15; 21:8).

With him the false prophet. The False Prophet (Revelation 13:11-18) will also be cast into the Lake of Fire. This is the third doom.

THE DOOM OF THE NATIONS (19:21)

VERSE 21

And the rest were killed with the sword which proceeded from the mouth of Him who sat on the horse. And all the birds were filled with their flesh.

And the rest (remnant) were killed (slain). This is the fourth doom, the doom of the nations. The kings of the earth, and their armies (Revelation 19:19) are slain. The word "slain" is apokteino and again, carries with it the idea of violence. The nations, who are slain, are not cast into the Lake of Fire at this time. They, as all the wicked prior to them, will be cast into Hell. They will be resurrected later to face the Great White Throne Judgment, and then cast into the Lake of Fire forever (Revelation 20:11-15).

With the sword which proceeded from the mouth of Him who sat on the horse. As we have already seen, this sword is the Word of God.

And all the birds were filled with their flesh. God always keeps His promises, even to the vultures of the air (Revelation 19:17-18). The word "fill" is chortazo, and means to "fill to overflowing."

REVELATION 20

THE MILLENIAL REIGN

SATAN BOUND ONE THOUSAND YEARS (20:1-3)

VERSE 1

Then I saw an angel coming down from heaven, having the key to the bottomless pit and a great chain in his hand.

Then I saw an angel coming down from heaven. This angel is not identified. Some believe that he is Michael, because it will be Michael that leads the angelic hosts against Satan as he attempts to destroy Israel during the Tribulation Period. It was also Michael that contended with Satan over the body of Moses (Jude 9).

Having the key to the bottomless pit. The word "key" symbolizes "access to." The "pit" is the word abyss and refers to a prison house in which billions of fallen angels (demons) were imprisoned after Satan was cast out of Heaven (Matthew 25:41, Luke 8:31, II Peter 2:4, and Jude 1:6).

And a great chain in his hand. The word "chain" is halusis and referred to "a chain used to bind the body of a prisoner." Paul wore a halusis in Rome (II Timothy 1:16), as did Peter in Jerusalem (Acts 12:6).

VERSE 2

He laid hold of the dragon, that serpent of old, who is the Devil and Satan, and bound him for a thousand years;

He laid hold of the dragon. "Laid hold of" is krateo and means "to seize by force." The "dragon" has already been identified as the Devil (Revelation 12:9).

That serpent of old who is the Devil and Satan. Again, there can be no mistake as to the identity of this prisoner.

And bound him for a thousand years. Satan is seized by the mighty angel, and bound with a "great chain" for a thousand years. It is in this passage that the "millennial" reign of Christ is described. The word "millennium" occurs nowhere in the Bible. It is a Latin word meaning one thousand years (mille=1000; annum=years). This is the only passage in the Bible that mentions a "thousand year" reign. But it is significant to note that in this passage, the thousand year span is mentioned six times (2-7). This passage is describing a literal, thousand year era in which the Lord Jesus Christ will rule the world (Jeremiah 30:9; Ezekiel 37:24-25; Hosea 3:5; and Luke 1:30-33).

VERSE 3

and he cast him into the bottomless pit, and shut him up, and set a seal on him, so that he should deceive the nations no more till the thousand years were finished. But after these things he must be released for a little while.

And he cast him into the bottomless pit. The Devil will be bound with a great chain, and cast (ballo, meaning "to throw down violently") into the bottomless pit, the prison house of demons. The bottomless pit (abyss) is feared by the demons. The demons in the Gadarene demoniac begged Jesus not to cast them into the deep (abyss), (Luke 8:31).

And shut him up, and set a seal on him. The phrase is literally "shut it and seal it." A seal will be placed to assure that he cannot escape.

So that he should deceive the nations no more. The Devil is a liar, and a master of deception. This is the area of his expertise. Following the Tribulation Period, in which he will deceive virtually the whole world, he will be bound in the bottomless pit.

Till the thousand years were finished. This is not the final doom of the Devil. It is but a brief term (Revelation 20:7).

But after these things he must be released for a little while/season. This is one of the saddest statements in the book of Revelation. After the thousand year reign of Jesus Christ on earth, Satan will be loosed for a "little season" to deceive the nations once more.

VERSE 4
And I saw thrones, and they sat on them, and judgment was committed to them. Then I saw the souls of those who had been beheaded for their witness to Jesus and for the word of God, who had not worshiped the beast or his image, and had not received his mark on their foreheads or on their hands. And they lived and reigned with Christ for a thousand years.

I saw thrones and they sat on them. After Satan is cast into the bottomless pit, John sees people sitting upon thrones on the earth. Those sitting upon the thrones are the saints of God. The Bible mentions three groups that will rule during the Millennial Kingdom. The first group will be resurrected Old Testament saints (Isaiah 26:19, and Daniel 12:2). The second group will be the apostles and the church (Matthew 19:28-29). The third group will be the Tribulation saints

(Revelation 7:14-15). This is a fulfillment of Matthew 19:28, Luke 22:30, and I Corinthians 6:3. Many from the nation of Israel will enter in the Millennial Kingdom: the 144,000 (Revelation 14:3-4); those who flee into the wilderness (Revelation 12:6); and those who remain in Jerusalem (Revelation 12:17). Millions of Gentiles who are saved during the Tribulation Period will enter into the kingdom (Revelation 7:9ff). But, no unsaved person will enter the Millenium. They will have all been destroyed at the Battle of Armageddon (Revelation 19:21). The Antichrist and False Prophet will have been cast into the Lake of Fire (Revelation 19:20). Satan will be bound in this passage, but many Old Testament passages describe this blessed era. From these passages, the following may be seen.

1. The promise of an earthly kingdom revolves around four covenants that God "cut" with Israel:

    Covenant with Abraham (Genesis 12:1-3). God promised Abraham the land of Palestine and that his seed would inhabit it forever. This fulfillment will be during the Millenium.

    Covenant with Moses (Deuteronomy 30:1-10). God promised Moses that in the end all Israel would be regathered and blessed in the land of Palestine. This fulfillment will be during the Millenium.

Covenant with David (II Samuel 7:16). God promised David that his house, throne and kingdom would be forever. This fulfillment will be during the Millennium when Christ, the Son of David will reign.

Covenant with Jeremiah (Jeremiah 31:31-34). God promised that in the last days Israel would be converted, and He would write His law upon their hearts. This fulfillment will be during the Millenium.

VERSE 5

But the rest of the dead did not live again until the thousand years were finished. This is the first resurrection.

But the rest of the dead did not live again until the thousand years were finished. This refers to the wicked dead. Their spirits are in Hades, and their bodies are still in the graves. The Bible teaches that there will be two resurrections of the dead. The first resurrection will be the resurrection of the righteous dead when Jesus comes to Rapture His church (I Thessalonians 4:13-18). The wicked dead will not be resurrected until after the Millennial Reign of Christ (Revelation 20:11-15). This is the second resurrection.

This is the first resurrection. The first resurrection is the resurrection of the righteous. These will reign with Christ during the Millennial Kingdom.

VERSE 6

Blessed and holy is he who has part in the first resurrection. Over such the second death has no power, but they shall be priests of God and of Christ, and shall reign with Him a thousand years.

Blessed and holy is he who has part in the first resurrection. This is the fifth of seven beatitudes found in the book of Revelation.

Over such the second death has no power. The "second death" is identified as the Lake of Fire in verse 14. The Lake of Fire is the eternal abode of the wicked. Those who have been born twice will die once but those who have only been born once will die twice (John 3:3-7).

But they shall be priests of God and of Christ. The redeemed of God are a kingdom of priests (Revelation 1:6). The priest had the blessed privilege of entering into the presence of God, and the awesome responsibility of interceding for others.

And shall reign with Him a thousand years. Not only are we priests, but we are kings. We will rule with Christ on this earth (Romans 8:17).

SATAN IS RELEASED (20:7-9)

VERSE 7

Now when the thousand years have expired, Satan will be released from his prison.

And when the thousand years have expired. After the Millennial Kingdom, Satan will be loosed out of the bottomless pit.

VERSE 8

and will go out to deceive the nations which are in the four corners of the earth, Gog and Magog, to gather them together to battle, whose number is as the sand of the sea.

And will go out to deceive the nations. The thousand year prison term has not rehabilitated the Devil. His nature is exactly as it was in the beginning in the Garden of Eden.

Gog and Magog, to gather them together to battle. This is taken from Ezekiel chapters thirty-eight and thirty-nine, where Gog and the land of Magog is predicted to launch an attack upon Israel, but he will be utterly destroyed by the

Messiah. As time went by, to the Jews, Gog and Magog came to represent everything that is wicked, and against God. After Satan is loosed, he will gather the nations of the world together one last time.

Whose number is as the sand of the sea. This shows what a master of deception the Devil is. All who enter into the Millennial Kingdom will be saints of God. However, over the course of a thousand years, multitudes of children will be born (Jeremiah 30:20, 31:29; Ezekiel 47:20; and Zechariah 10:8). They will be unregernarate, and will serve Christ, not because they choose to, but because they will have no option since Satan has been bound. They will be able to sin, and will become part of Satan's rebellion. The Millennial Reign of Christ illustrates two things. First, living in a perfect environment does not make a sinner into a saint. Those born during the Millennial Kingdom will have a perfect environment, and yet they still rebel against God. Second, having a perfect heredity does not make a sinner into a saint. Those born during this period will all have godly parents, and they will still revel against God. God created man with a will because He wanted us to serve Him because we love Him, and choose to serve Him. During the Millenium, Christ will rule the world with a "rod of iron." At the end of the

Millennial Reign, God will give all those born during this period the opportunity to choose evil if that is what they desire to do.

VERSE 9

They went up on the breadth of the earth and surrounded the camp of the saints and the beloved city. And fire came down from God out of heaven and devoured them.

They went up on the breadth of the earth. This army of Satan will be spread over the entire earth.

And surrounded the camp of the saints and the beloved city. The saints of God are here pictured encamped about their beloved city of Jerusalem to stand in its defense against the enemies of God.

And fire came down from God out of heaven. Fire has often been used by God as an instrument of Divine judgment, for example, Sodom and Gomorrah, the Egyptian plagues, etc. (Genesis 19:24; Exodus 9:23; Numbers 11:1, 16:35; Psalms 105:4; and II Peter 3:12). This fire is rained down from the heavens by God Almighty.

And devoured them. The Greek work for "devour" is kataphago and means "to consume by eating up." The enemies of God will be utterly destroyed. There will be no sign of them left. This is the fifth doom, the doom of Gog and Magog.

THE DOOM OF SATAN (20:10)

VERSE 10

The devil, who deceived them, was cast into the lake of fire and brimstone where the beast and the false prophet are. And they will be tormented day and night forever and ever.

The devil, who deceived them, was cast into the lake of fire. This is the sixth doom. Here, the final end of the Devil is described. He will be cast into the Lake of Fire. It is interesting to note that from the beginning to end; his nature has remained the same. He is the master of deception.

Where the beast and the false prophet are. In Revelation 19:20, the "Beast" (Antichrist), and the False Prophet were cast into the Lake of Fire. Over a thousand years have now expired, and they are still there. The time has now come for their leader, Satan, to join them.

And they will be tormented day and night. The "Lake of Fire" is a place of torment. There is no rest for those who enter its domain, only torment.

Forever and ever. The phrase is literally "unto the age of the ages." This is the strongest Greek expression for eternity.

THE DOOM OF THE WICKED (20:11-15)

VERSE 11

Then I saw a great white throne and Him who sat on it, from whose face the earth and the heaven fled away. And there was found no place for them.

Then I saw a great white throne. Verses 11-15 contain the seventh and final doom – the doom of the wicked. We have already seen the Throne of God in the book of Revelation (4:4, 20:4). Here, additional information is given concerning this throne. First, it is a "great" throne. The word "great" is megas and means "mighty." Second, it is a "white" throne. As we have already seen several times in our study of Revelation, "white" is often used to symbolize purity and holiness (Psalms 9:1, 97:2; and Daniel 7:9).

And Him who sat on it. The great judge seated upon the throne is the Lord Jesus Christ (John 5:22).

From whose face the earth and the heaven fled away. The Bible frequently refers to the time when this present world will pass away (Psalms 102:25-27, Isaiah 51:6, Matthew 24:35,

Mark 13:31, and II Peter 3:10). It is probably at this time, after the Great White Throne Judgment, that the present heavens and earth will be destroyed, and replaced by the new heaven and earth.

There was found no place for them. There will be no place in the new age for this old sin-cursed world.

VERSE 12

And I saw the dead, small and great, standing before God, and books were opened. And another book was opened, which is the Book of Life. And the dead were judged according to their works, by the things which were written in the books.

And I saw the dead, small and great. The word "dead" is nekros, and here, as in Matthew 8:22' John 5:25; Ephesians 2:1, 5:14; Philippians 3:11, and Colossians 2:13, refers to those who are "spiritually dead." This is the judgment of the unsaved. All the lost, regardless of their station in life ("small and great") will be judged by Jesus. The Lord Jesus will either be our Savior, or our Judge!

Standing before God. They stand before the Lord Jesus awaiting judgment, as a convicted criminal awaits his sentence.

And books were opened. These books contain the life history of those standing before the Throne. Every deed has been recorded in books in Heaven, and will be used against them in the judgment (Daniel 7:10, and Malachi 3:16).

And another book was opened, which is the Book of Life. The "Book of Life" contains the names of all the redeemed of God (Exodus 32:32, Daniel 12:1, Luke 10:20, Philippians 4:3, Hebrews 12:23, and Revelation 21:27). The "Book of Life" will not be here to determine if any of these will be saved, but will be here as evidence that they are not. Jesus said that in the Day of Judgment, "many will say to me...Lord, Lord, have we not prophesied in your name?" (Matthew 7:21-23). Many who are lost will think that they are saved, but the "Book of Life" will reveal that they are not.

… According to their works… God is Just. All of the wicked will be judged according to what they have done. Every deed has been recorded in "the books." All through life, they have been writing their own destiny. They will be condemned by the record they themselves have kept.

VERSE 13

The sea gave up the dead who were in it, and Death and Hades delivered up the dead who were in them. And they were judged, each one according to his works.

The sea gave up the dead who were in it. This phrase expressed the truth that all the wicked will be raised to stand judgment. Even those who have been lost in the depths of the sea are known to God, and will be raised to give an account of their life to God.

Death and Hades delivered up the dead who were in them. The word "Hell" is "Hades," and refers to the "region of departed spirits of the lost." Again, the idea here is that not a one of the wicked will escape this judgment.

And they were judged, each one according to his works. Again, the emphasis is that they will be judged according to what they have done. This is the consistent teaching of the scriptures (Matthew 16:27, Romans 2:6, I Corinthians 3:13, II Corinthians 5:10, I Peter 1:17, and Revelation 2:23).

VERSE 14

Then Death and Hades were cast into the lake of fire. This is the second death.

Then Death and Hades (hell) were cast into the lake of fire. The last enemy to be defeated will be death (I Corinthians 15:26). The word "hell," again is "Hades." Death claims the "body" of the lost. Hades claims the "soul" of the lost, and is the intermediate place of punishment for the wicked until they are raised at the Great White Throne. After this judgment, they will be cast into the "Lake of Fire" which is the eternal place of torment for the lost.

This is the second death. The first death is "physical death." The "second death" is an eternity spent in the Lake of Fire (Revelation 2:11, 20:6. 21:8).

VERSE 15

And anyone not found written in the Book of Life was cast into the lake of fire.

And anyone not found written in the Book of Life. This is the final epitaph! This is the final writing on the subject! Anyone whose name is not written in the "Book of Life" will be cast into the "Lake of Fire." The "Book of Life" is God's record of those who have eternal life (Exodus 32:32-33; Philippians 4:3, and Revelation 3:5, 13:8, 17:8, 20:12 & 15; 21:27; 22:19). The only way to have eternal life is through

Jesus (John 3:16; II Corinthians 5:19; I Timothy 2:6; Hebrews 2:9; and I John 2:2).

REVELATION

THE NEW HEAVEN AND EARTH (21:1-9)

VERSE 1

Now I saw a new heaven and a new earth, for the first heaven and earth had passed away. Also there was no more sea.

Now I saw a new heaven and a new earth. This is a fulfillment of Isaiah 65:17. It has been a long, sometimes dark journey through the book of Revelation. We have traced the history of the church from its beginning to its Laodicean period. We have journeyed through the terror-filled days of the Tribulation Period. We have seen the seven dooms of the enemies of God, and now we are about to see the bliss of the saved. The word "new" is kainos, and means "new in quality." In the Bible, there are three heavens mentioned. There is the atmospheric heaven that envelops the earth, and it is referred to as the "first heaven." The stars and planets comprise the "second heaven." The "third heaven" is where God dwells (II Corinthians 12). The word John uses here for heaven is ouranos, and refers to the atmosphere around the earth.

For the first heaven and first earth had passed away. In II Peter 3:10, we read that the earth will pass away with a thunderous crash. This will probably be accomplished as the gasses in the atmosphere explode, purifying the heavens of any deadly germ that might cause disease or death.

Also there was no more sea. In Bible days, the people hated the "sea." The seas were a barrier to the nations of the world, because they were not navigable. The "sea" is also used to refer to the "storminess and restlessness" of the nations of the world. The idea is that in the new earth there will be no barriers to prevent us from enjoying all that God has created for us. There also will be no restlessness, for this will be an eternity in perfect peace.

VERSE 2

Then I, John, saw the holy city, New Jerusalem, coming down out of heaven from God, prepared as a bride adorned for her husband.

Then I, John, saw the holy city, New Jerusalem, coming down out of heaven from God. The "new earth" must have a "new capital." This capital is in sharp contrast to the former world capital, "Babylon" (Revelation 17; 18). This capital is "holy" and is the city that Abraham looked for (Hebrews 11:10), and that Jesus promised us in John 14.

Prepared as a bride adorned for her husband. The groom anxiously awaits the arrival of his bride. When she appears, she is the most beautiful sight he has ever seen. This is the symbolism here. The Holy City, which God prepared for His children, will exceed all our expectations (II Corinthians 2:9).

VERSE 3

And I heard a loud voice from heaven saying, "Behold, the tabernacle of God is with men, and He will dwell with them, and they shall be His people. God Himself will be with them and be their God.

And I heard a loud voice from heaving saying. This voice is probably that of one of the "angels of the presence" (Revelation 16:17, 19:5).

Behold the tabernacle of God is with men. The "Tabernacle" was where the Shekinah Glory was, which represented the presence of God to the people of Israel (Exodus 40:34-38).

He will dwell with them and they shall be His people. The word "dwell" is skenoo, and literally means "to pitch a tent."

God Almighty will "pitch His tent among us." The idea is that He is coming to live with us on earth.

VERSE 4

"And God will wipe away every tear from their eyes; there shall be no more death, nor sorrow, nor crying. There shall be no more pain, for the former things have passed away."

God will wipe away every tear from their eyes. When the earth is made new, some drastic changes will take place. There will be no more tears, for there will be no cause to weep. There will be no death, no sorrow no pain.

The former things have passed away. The former earth was cursed by sin, and characterized by pain, suffering, death, and sorrow. But, all these things have now "passed away."

VERSE 5

Then He who sat on the throne said, "Behold, I make all things new. From the description that follows, it is obvious that the one sitting upon the Throne is the Lord Jesus.

Write, for these words are true and faithful. John can hardly believe what he has seen, a world not cursed by sin. Jesus turns to him and says, "Yes, John, what you are seeing is true. I have made all things new. Go ahead and write it down, for it is true!"

VERSE 6

And He said to me, "It is done! I am the Alpha and the Omega, the Beginning and the End. I will give of the fountain of the water of life freely to him who thirsts.

And He said to me, It is done! Again, all God has to do is speak, and His will is accomplished.

I am the Alpha and the Omega, the Beginning and the End Alpha and Omega. Alpha and Omega are the first and last letters of the Greek alphabet. The alphabet is man's way of storing his accumulated knowledge. Jesus is the sum-total of all knowledge, from "A" to "Z" - He is omniscient.

Jesus is also the "beginning and the end" - He is omnipresent. He is and always has been at all places at all times. He had no beginning and will have no ending.

I will give of the fountain of the water of life freely to him who thirsts. This is the fulfillment of Isaiah 55:1, and Revelation 7:17. This "water of life" is given to us "freely." The word "freely" is dorean and means "gratis, or without a cause." All of God's benefits to us are the result of His amazing grace (Ephesians 2:8)!

VERSE 7

"He who overcomes shall inherit all things, and I will be his God and he shall be My son.

He who overcomes shall inherit all things. The "overcomer" in John's writings is the true child of God (John 16:33; I John 4:4, 5:4; and Revelation 2:7, 11, 17, 26; 3:5, 12, 21). The children of God will inherit all things.

And He shall be My son. The basis upon which we inherit all things is that we are God's "son." We are the rightful heirs (Romans 8:17).

VERSE 8

"But the cowardly, unbelieving, abominable, murderers, sexually immoral, sorcerers, idolaters, and all liars shall have their part in the lake which burns with fire and brimstone, which is the second death."

But. We are about to see the sharp contrast between the blessing of the saved, and the doom of the wicked.

The cowardly (fearful). The word is deilia and occurs only here and in Matthew 8:26, and Mark 4:40. The words refers to a "coward," and here means those who are afraid to take a stand of Christ (Matthew 10:32-33).

Unbelieving. The word is apistos and means "faithless."

The abominable. The word is bdeluktos and refers to "those who deceive others by professing to know God, when in reality they don't (Titus 1:16).

Murderers. This refers to those who take the lives of others. Jesus expanded it by saying that whoever hates his brother is a murderer (Matthew 5:21-22, and I John 3:15).

Sexually immoral (whoremongers). The word is pornois and refers to "illicit sexual intercourse of all types."

Sorcerers. The word is pharmakia and refers to "drug users, and traffickers."

Idolaters. The word is eidololatria and means "those who are enslaved to any god other than Jehovah."

Liars. The word is pseudes, and refers to anything that is "false," not just spoke falsehoods.

Shall have their part in the lake which burns with fire and brimstone. The above list is not to be taken as all-inclusive (Galatians 5:19-21). This is just a partial description of those whose fleshly appetites have not been conquered by Christ.

VERSE 9

Then one of the seven angels who had the seven bowls filled with the seven last plagues came to me and talked with me, saying, "Come, I will show you the bride, the Lamb's wife."

Then one of the seven angels who had the seven bowls. It was one of these very angels that had shown John the great harlot, Babylon (Revelation 17). Now one of them shows him the Bride, the Lamb's wife.

THE NEW JERUSALEM (21:10-27)

VERSE 10

And he carried me away in the Spirit to a great and high mountain, and showed me the great city, the holy Jerusalem, descending out of heaven from God.

And he carried me away in the Spirit to a great and high mountain. In Revelation 3:17 the angel carried John away in the spirit to a desert to see the great whore. Here, he is taken to a majestic mountain peak to view the chaste Bride of Christ. What a contrast!

And showed me the great city, the holy Jerusalem. This is the same description given of the city in Revelation 21:2.

Descending out of heaven from God. God is the builder and architect of this great city (Hebrews 11:10).

VERSE 11
having the glory of God. Her light was like a most precious stone, like a jasper stone, clear as crystal.

Having the glory of God. The idea is that God's very presence (glory) is in the Holy City.

Her light was like a most precious stone. The word "light" is phoster and means "luminary, or that which reflects light." The reflection of this city is like a most precious (costly) stone glistening in the brilliant sunlight. The city reflects the glory of Almighty God who is in its midst.

Like a jasper stone, clear as crystal. The word "jasper" is iaspis and does not refer to the modern stone that we know by that name. This jasper was "clear as crystal," and was obviously a diamond.

VERSE 12
Also she had a great and high wall with twelve gate, and twelve angels at the gates, and names written on them, which are the names of the twelve tribes of the children of Israel:

She had a great and high wall. In Bible days, each city had a great wall around it to protect it from enemies. The wall represented security and safety to its inhabitants. There is no need for protection from the enemies of God, for they are all in the Lake of Fire. But, John uses this symbolism to describe the city as a place of safety and security.

With twelve gates. The "twelve gates" symbolize free and easy access into and out of the city. The idea here is that the walls in no way will restrict the inhabitants of this holy city.

And twelve angels at the gates. Angels are described as "ministering spirits sent forth to minister to them who are the heirs of salvation (Hebrews 1:14). The idea is probably that the angels are at the gates to minister to the saints of God as they go in and out of the city.

And names written on them...the twelve tribes of the children of Israel. This is the fulfillment of Ezekiel 48:31. The names of the twelve tribes of Israel appear, one on each of the twelve gates. This is probably to serve as a reminder to us that we have received our Scriptures, our Savior, and much, much more from the Jews. "Salvation of the Jews" (John 4:22).

VERSE 13

three gates on the east, three gates on the north, three gates on the south, and three gates on the west.

Three gates. Just as there is order in this present world, there will be order in the new world. There will be three gates on each side of the city. This again, illustrates ease and access into and out of the city.

VERSE 14

Now the wall of the city had twelve foundations, and on them were the names of the twelve apostles of the Lamb.

The wall of the city had twelve foundations. The strength of any structure depends on its foundation. The walls of the Holy City have twelve foundations. There is no danger of it ever falling.

On them were the names of the twelve apostles. The doctrine of the apostles was the foundation upon which the church was built. In the Holy City, the apostles will be honored by having their names written upon the foundations of the walls of the city. It is doubtful that the name of Judas will be listed, for Jesus said that he was never really one of the twelve, but "a devil from the beginning" (John 6:70). In Acts 1:23-26, the early church selected Matthias to replace

Judas. However, nothing is ever heard of him after this and it could also be noted that he was selected by a questionable process, the casting of lots. It is possible that the early church acted hastily in selecting Matthias, and that God intended for Paul to be the twelfth apostle (Acts 9:15).

VERSE 15
And he who talked with me had a gold reed to measure the city, its gates, and its wall.

And he who talked with me had a gold reed to measure the city. The "vial angel" who was responsible for showing John around the city, had a "reed" which he used to measure.

VERSE 16
The city is laid out as a square; its length is as great as its breadth. And he measured the city with the reed: twelve thousand furlongs. Its length, breadth, and height are equal.

The city is laid out as a square. The city is a cube which in scripture is used to refer to that which is perfect. The altar of burnt offering, and the altar of incense were cubs (Exodus 27:1 & 30:2). The Holy of Holies in Solomon's Temple was a cube, twenty cubits each way (I Kings6:20). The High Priest's breastplate was a cube (Exodus 27:1 & 28:16).

Twelve thousand furlongs. The word "furlong" is stade. Each side of the city was 1500 miles long. The total area of the city is 2,250,000 square miles. The Jews dreamed of a rebuilt Jerusalem that would reach to Damascus, but they never dreamed of a city of this magnitude. This city today would stretch nearly from London to New York.

VERSE 17

Then he measured its wall: one hundred and forty-four cubits, according to the measure of a man, that is, of an angel.

He measured its wall: one hundred and forty-four cubits. The height of the wall is about 220 feet high. This was not considered a high wall in Bible days. The walls of ancient Babylon were over 300 feet high. There is no comparison between the walls of the city and the height of the city itself. The symbolism seems to be that high walls are not needed, because they are not for the purpose of defense, all the enemies of God are ł (in) the Lake of Fire.

According to the measure of a man, that is, of an angel. Even though the measurement is taken by an angel, the standard used is man's cubit, about eighteen inches.

VERSE 18

The construction of its wall was of jasper; and the city was pure gold, like clear glass.

The construction of its wall was of jasper. The walls are made of "Jasper" (diamond), clear as crystal.

And the city was pure gold, like clear glass. The city, which measured 1500 square miles, is constructed of "pure gold," the most precious of all metals.

VERSE 19

The foundations of the wall of the city were adorned with all kinds of precious stones: the first foundation was jasper, the second sapphire, the third chalcedony, the fourth emerald.

The foundations of the wall of the city were adorned with all kinds of precious stones. The twelve foundations of the wall are as lavish as the city itself. We have already seen that they are inscribed with the names of the twelve apostles. Here, we see that they are "garnished" (adorned) with all kinds of precious stones. One cannot be dogmatic about the identity of the twelve stones listed, but each of these stones contributes to the unimaginable beauty of this Holy City.

The first foundation was jasper. As we have already seen, this was probably a diamond.

The second sapphire. The sapphire was a brilliant blue stone.

The third chalcedony. This was a green stone found in the copper mines near Chalcedon.

The fourth emerald. The emerald was the greenest of all stones.

VERSE 20

the fifth sardonyx, the sixth sardius, the seventh chrysolite, the eighth beryl, the ninth topaz, the tenth chrysoprase, the eleventh jacinth, and the twelfth amethyst.

The fifth, sardonyx. This was a stone that was white, with layers of red and brown.

The sixth, sardius. This was the most common of the stones listed here. It was blood-red.

The seventh, chrysolite. This stone was probably gold colored. It is mentioned also in Exodus 28:20.

The eighth, beryl. This stone was similar to the emerald.

The ninth, a topaz. The topaz was a transparent greenish-gold stone and was very valuable.

The tenth, a chrysoprase. This was also a greenish-gold stone.

The eleventh, a jacinth. This was a violet-colored stone.

The twelfth, an amethyst. This was similar to the jacinth, but more brilliant.

VERSE 21

The twelve gates were twelve pearls: each individual gate was of one pearl. And the street of the city was pure gold, like transparent glass.

The twelve gates were twelve pearls. Each of the twelve gates into the city is a giant pearl. The pearl is created when a foreign object enters the oyster, and wounds its flesh. The oyster dies trying to protect itself from this foreign object, and in the process, a beautiful pearl is created. In Matthew 13:46, Jesus is referred to as the "pearl of great price." The only way into this Holy City is through Jesus (John 10:9 & 14:6); there is none other name under heaven whereby we must be saved (Acts 4:12). The gates of pearl will be a constant reminder of the great price Jesus paid in order for us to have access into the city of God (I Peter 1:18-19)

And the street of the city was pure gold. Even the streets in the city are made of pure gold.

VERSE 22

But I saw no temple in it, for the Lord God Almighty and the Lamb are it temple.

But I saw no temple in it. The glory of ancient Jerusalem was the Temple. John looks all around New Jerusalem for the Temple, but discovers that there is no Temple in the city.

For the Lord God Almighty and the Lamb are it temple. The Temple was the visible representation of the presence of God on earth. In this new earth there is no need for a Temple, for God, Himself and the Lamb will dwell here on earth with the saints (Revelation 21:3).

VERSE 23

The city had no need of the sun or of the moon to shine in it, for the glory of God illuminated it. The Lamb is its light.

The city had no need of the sun or of the moon. The sun and moon were created to provide light for planet earth (Genesis 1:14-19). In the new earth, they will no longer be needed.

For the glory of God illuminated it...the Lamb is its light. The reason the sun and moon are no longer needed is that now the presence of God is on earth. The Shekinah glory of God far exceeds that of the sun or the moon, and it will illuminate the new earth. In our physical bodies, we cannot behold the glory of God, but in our resurrected bodies, we will behold Him as He is (I John 3:2).

VERSE 24
And the nations of those who are saved shall walk in its light, and the kings of the earth bring their glory and honor into it.

And the nations of those who are saved shall walk in its light. This does not mean that there will be nations on earth that are not saved. All the unsaved have been cast into the Lake of Fire (Revelation 20:12-15). The idea here is that all the nations of the earth will be saved, and will live in the midst of His glory.

And the kings of the earth bring their glory and honor. All the glory and honor of all the ages combined will be nothing compared to the glory of God present in the New Jerusalem.

VERSE 25
Its gates shall not be shut at all by day (there shall be no night there).

Its gates shall not be shut at all by day. The gates of an ancient city were usually kept open during the day, in order to allow access into and out of the city. They were closed at night, to prevent the enemy from entering.

There shall be no night there. Darkness is used in the Bible to refer to that which is evil (John 12:35; Romans 13:12, and I John 1:4-10). There will be no evil in the New Jerusalem, therefore, there will be no need for the gates of the city to be closed. The picture is that of a city perfectly safe and secure, eternally bathed in the light of God's glory.

VERSE 26

And they shall bring the glory and the honor of the nations into it.

Glory and the honor of the nations. This is a reiteration of verse twenty-four. The city of God will have the best of all the nations (Isaiah 60:4, 11).

VERSE 27

But there shall by no means enter it anything that defiles, or causes an abomination or a lie, but only those who are written in the Lamb's Book of Life.

There shall by no means... Here the double negative is again used for emphasis.

Enter it anything that defiles. Again, the safety and security of the city is described. Nothing that could ever defile the city will be allowed to enter into it. All that could defile it is now in the Lake of Fire (Revelation 20:15 & 21:8).

Only those who are written in the Lamb's Book of Life. The only basis upon which one may enter into the City of God is by having their name in the Book of Life. The "Book of Life" is God's record of those who have eternal life (Exodus 32:32-33; Philippians 4:3; Revelation3:5, 13:8, 17:8, 20:12, 15; 21:27 & 22:19). The only way to have eternal life is through Jesus (John 3:16; II Corinthians 5:19; I Timothy 2:6; Hebrews 2:9, and I John 2:2).

THE RIVER OF LIFE (22:1)

VERSE 1

And he showed me a pure river of water of life, clear as crystal, proceeding from the throne of God and of the Lamb.

And he showed me a pure river of water of life. There was a River of Life in the Garden of Eden (Genesis 2:10). In the vision of Ezekiel, he saw a river flowing from the Temple of God (Ezekiel 47:1-12). Water is often used in the Bible to symbolize life (Psalms 36:10; Proverbs 10:11, 13:14, 14:27, 16:22; Jeremiah 2:13; Joel 3:8; John 4:14, 7:38; and Revelation 7:17, 21:6 & 22:17). Those who drink of the River of Life are immortal and will never die. During the Tribulation Period, the rivers become "blood" (Revelation 8:10, and 16:4), but in the Holy City, they are pure, and "clear as crystal."

Proceeding from the throne of God and of the Lamb. In Heaven the River of Life will serve as a constant reminder to us that the source of "life" is God. It was God who created man in the beginning (Genesis 2), and it was God that made it possible for man to have eternal life (Ephesians 2:8).

THE TREE OF LIFE (22:2)

VERSE 2

In the middle of its street and on either side of the river, was the tree of life, which bore twelve fruits, each tree yielding its fruit every month. The leaves of the tree were for the healing of the nations.

In the middle of its street. This phrase is probably connected with verse one. The street is a two-lane street with the beautiful River of Life flowing between the two lanes. As we have already seen, the street is pure gold (Revelation 21:21).

On either side of the river was the tree of life. In the Garden of Eden there was only one Tree of Life mentioned (Genesis 3:3, 24). In the eternal Holy City, it appears that there will be many. John sees the Trees of Life lining the banks of the River of Life which proceeded from the Throne of God.

Which bore twelve fruits each tree yielding its fruit each month. After the fall of man in the Garden of Eden, God placed cherubim with flaming swords by the Tree of Life to prevent man from eating of its fruit (Genesis 3:24). The Tree of Life was the source of eternal life (Genesis 3:22). In the Holy City, man will once again access to the fruit of the tree. In our present age, certain fruits are only available at certain seasons. But in the Holy City, the fruit of the Tree of Life will be available "every month."

The leaves of the tree were for the healing of the nations. Many of our present-day medicines are made from various herbs and leaves. The "leaves" of the Tree of Life are not intended as a "cure," for sickness, disease, and death have already been annihilated from the new heaven and earth (Revelation 21:4, and 21:27). Quite the opposite, they preserve the health of the inhabitants of the Holy City.

GOD SHALL DWELL WITH MAN (22:3-5)

VERSE 3

And there shall be no more curse, but the throne of God and of the Lamb shall be in it, and His servants shall serve him.

There shall be no more curse. When a man sinned, God placed a curse on the earth (Genesis 3:14). Over the ages, man has had to live in a sin-cursed world. But, in the new world to come, the curse will be removed for there will be no more sin.

But the throne of God and of the Lamb shall be in it. The curse prevented God from dwelling in the midst of man. But, in the Holy City, the curse will be replaced by the very presence of Almighty God. What a contrast!

And His servants shall serve him. John now describes the blessed condition of those who inhabit the Holy City. First, they shall "serve" God. The word "serve" is latreuo, and means to "worship." They will spend eternity worshipping God. True worship is a beautiful thing. Much of what we call worship today, is not. Worship is the inevitable response of one who has been overwhelmed by the presence and power of Almighty God.

VERSE 4

They shall see His face, and His name shall be on their foreheads.

They shall see His face. In Bible days, women often wore veils over their faces, to conceal their identity. To see the face of a person was to know their identity. The second blessing of the inhabitants of the Holy City is that they will know God as He actually is. In this age, we can only get glimpses of His majesty and glory. But, on (one) day, we will see Him as He is (1 Corinthians 13:12, and 1 John 3:2).

His name shall be on their foreheads. This symbolizes ownership. The third blessing of the inhabitants of the Holy City is that there will be no doubt as to who they belong to.

VERSE 5

There shall be no night there: They need no lamp nor light of the sun, for the Lord God gives them light. And they shall reign forever and ever.

There shall be no night there. The sun and the moon were created to provide light for planet earth (Genesis 1:14-19). In the new earth, they will no longer be needed. The reason the sun and moon are no longer needed, is that now the presence of God is on earth. The Glory of God far exceeds that of the sun or the moon. The glory of God will illuminate the new earth. In our physical bodies, we cannot behold the glory of God (1 Corinthians 13:12), but in our resurrected bodies, we will behold Him as He is (1 John 3:2).

They shall reign forever and ever. The fourth blessing of the redeemed is that they will "reign" with Christ eternally. The phrase "forever and ever," literally means "unto the age of the ages." It is the strongest Greek phrase to describe eternity. With this statement, John concludes his description of the Holy City.

CONCLUDING WORDS (22:6-21)

VERSE 6

Then he said to me, "These words are faithful and true." And the Lord God of the holy prophets sent His angel to show His servants the things which must shortly take place.

These words are faithful and true. The things which John has seen and heard have been almost too glorious to believe. The angel says, "Go ahead, write them down, they are faithful and true."

And the Lord God of the holy prophets. The author of the "Revelation" is the same God that the Old Testament prophets worshiped.

Things which must shortly take place. This is the first of four times in these concluding verses that we are reminded of the imminent return of the Lord Jesus Christ to the earth.

VERSE 7

Behold, I am coming quickly! Blessed is he who keeps the words of the prophecy of this book."

Blessed is he who keeps the words…of this book. This is the sixth of seven beatitudes. It is a reiteration of the first one found in chapter one, verse three.

I come quickly. "Quickly" is tachu and again reminds us of the imminence of Christ's return for His church at the Rapture.

VERSE 8

Now I, John, saw and heard theses things. And when I heard and saw, I fell down to worship before the feet of the angel who showed me these things.

I John saw and heard these things. John gives his own testimony that the things contained in the book are true.

I fell down to worship before the feet of the angel. John has already made this mistake once (Revelation 19:10).

VERSE 9

Then he said to me, "See that you do not do that. For I am your fellow servant, and of your brethren the prophets, and of those who keep the words of this book. Worship God."

See that you do not do that. The angel's reply is the same as it was before (Revelation 19:10).

Worship God. The phrase "worship God" is in the aorist imperative, and literally means "worship God only!"

VERSE 10

And he said to me, "Do not seal the words of the prophecy of this book, for the times is at hand."

Do not seal the words of the prophecy. Daniel received a revelation similar to John's, but was commanded to "seal it" (Daniel 12:4). John is told not to seal his visions. For many, the book of Revelation is a deep, dark, mysterious book. However, God never intended for it to be so. The title of the book is "Revelation," which means an "unveiling." The book was written to reveal to us God's plan for the future. If the book of Revelation is taken at face value, and interpreted in the light of its Old Testament background, its truths can be understood by any child of God.

For the time is at hand. The reason the book is not to be sealed is because it is describing events that are already beginning to happen.

VERSE 11

"He who is unjust, let him be unjust still; he who is filthy, let him be filthy still; he who is righteous, let him be righteous still; he who is holy, let him be holy still."

He who is unjust let him be unjust still. Since the Lord Jesus Christ's coming is at hand, we should be ready. Those who are not ready when He comes will not have a second chance. Those who are unjust will remain unjust throughout eternity.

He who is righteous, let him be righteous still. On the positive side, those who are righteous will be eternally righteous.

VERSE 12
"And behold, I am coming quickly, and My reward is with Me, to give to every one according to his work."

Behold I come quickly. This is the third reference in these concluding verses to the imminent return of Christ.

My reward is with Me. When He returns, He will reward those who are righteous (Hebrews 11:6). Rewards are always based upon our works (Romans 2:6 and 1 Peter 1:17).

To give to every one according to his work. Salvation is by grace. There is nothing that we can do to merit it. But, our eternal rewards will be determined by our actions and deeds (Romans 2:26; II Corinthians 5:10; and Revelation 2:23).

VERSE 13
"I am the Alpha and the Omega, the Beginning and the End, the First and the Last."

Alpha and Omega. Alpha and Omega are the first and last letters of the Greek alphabet. The alphabet is man's way of storing his accumulated knowledge. Jesus is the sum-total of all knowledge, from "A" to "Z". Jesus is omniscient.

The beginning and the end. Jesus is Omnipresent. He is and always has been at all places at all times. He had no beginning and will have no ending. He is the eternal God.

VERSE 14

Blessed are those who do His commandments, that they may have the right to the tree of life, and may enter through the gates into the city.

Blessed are those who do His commandments. This is the seventh and final beatitude in the book of Revelation. The best manuscripts read "wash their robes" rather than "do His commandments". Either way, the truth is the same. Only those who have been washed in the blood of the Lamb are able to "do His commandments".

That they may have the right to the tree of life. Access to the Tree of Life assures one of eternal life.

May enter through the gates into the city. Only those who have been blood-washed will be allowed access into the Holy City.

VERSE 15

But outside are dogs and sorcerers and sexually immoral and murderers and idolaters, and whoever loves and practices a lie.

But outside (for without, KJV). "Without/outside" does not mean that the wicked are "outside" the walls of the city milling around. They are all in the Lake of fire (Revelation 21:8) and will never be allowed into the city.

Dogs and sorcerers and sexually immoral…This is the same description given of the wicked in Revelation 21:8. Here, "dogs" is added, not literal dogs, but the morally impure (Deuteronomy 23:18; II Kings 8:13; Psalms 22:17 & 21; Matthew 7:6; Mark 7:27; and Philippians 3:3). Dogs in the Bible days were scavengers, and were held in utmost contempt. The Jew referred to the Gentiles as "dogs", because they were considered to be unclean.

VERSE 16

"I, Jesus, have sent My angel to testify to you these things in the churches. I am the Root and the Offspring of David, the Bright and Morning Star."

I, Jesus, have sent My angel to testify. This is the final attestation as to the source of the Revelation that John has seen.

In the churches. This is the first time the word "church" has occurred since chapter three. All during the Tribulation Period, there is no mention of the church, since it is in heaven with the Lord.

I am the Root and the Offspring of David. The Lord Jesus here shows His divine right to sit upon the throne as King of Kings, and Lord of Lords. He is the offspring of David (Luke 1:32). This is also a way of expressing His eternality. Jesus is not only the offspring of David, but He is the "root" from which David sprang.

The Bright and Morning Star. This is a reference to Jesus. The morning star is the star that rises at dawn when it is darkest. This is probably a reference to His Second Coming. At the darkest hour, Jesus will come. The Davidic King is called a star in Numbers 24:17 and Luke 1:78. Jesus is also called the "daystar" in II Peter 1:19.

VERSE 17

The Spirit and the bride say, "Come!" And let him who hears say, "Come!" And let him who thirsts come. Whoever desires, let him take the water of life freely.

And the Spirit and the bride say, "Come!" This is the final invitation written in the Scriptures. It is issued by the Holy Spirit and the church, the "Bride of Christ."

And let him who hears say, "Come!" Those who hear the invitation, and come to Christ, have a responsibility to issue the invitation to others.

And let him who thirsts come…take the water of life freely. As we have already seen, Jesus is the "Water of Life." Those who are thirsty may drink freely.

VERSE 18

For I testify to everyone who hears the words of the prophecy of this book: If anyone adds to these things, God will add to him the plagues that are written in this book;

For I testify to everyone. These words appear to come from the apostle John.

If anyone adds to these things. It was not uncommon in the ancient world for a writer to add a stern warning such as this at the end. Similar warnings are found in other places in the Bible (Deuteronomy 4:2; and Proverbs 30:5-6). The idea here is that no one is to add to the teachings found in this book.

God will add to him the plagues that are written in this book. The warning is indeed severe. The agent of this severe judgment is God, Himself. We have already seen the severity of the plagues poured out by God upon the earth during the Tribulation Period.

VERSE 19

and if anyone takes away from the words of the book of this prophecy, God shall take away his part from the Book of Life, from the holy city, and from the things which are written in this book.

If anyone takes away from the words of the book of this prophecy. Not only is the prophecy which John has received not to be added to, but, nothing which God has revealed to him is to be deleted.

God shall take away his part from the Book of Life. This phrase is not to be taken to mean that the one who does this will lose their salvation, but that those who would knowingly pervert the Truth of God are not really believers.

VERSE 20

He who testifies to these things says, "Surely I am coming quickly." Amen. Even so, come, Lord Jesus!

He who testifies to these things says. As we have already seen in chapter one, this revelation is from the Lord Jesus Christ (Revelation 1:1). "These things" refers to the prophecies which John had received in the book of Revelation.

Surely I am coming quickly. His promise is "I come quickly." The last recorded words of our Lord Jesus contain both pathos and glory. Jesus' coming will bring judgment upon the sinner and glory to the redeemed!

VERSE 21

The grace of our Lord Jesus Christ be with you all. Amen.

The grace of our Lord Jesus Christ be with you all. How fitting it is that the Bible ends with the word "grace." This is the final word! Man sinned, and became a creature totally depraved, and alienated from God. "But God, who is rich in mercy, for His great love wherewith He loved us, even when we were dead in sins, has quickened us together with Christ, (by grace you are saved) and has raised us up together, and made us sit together in heavenly places in Christ Jesus: that in the ages to come he might shew the exceeding riches of His grace in His kindness toward us through Christ Jesus. "For by grace are you saved through faith; and that not of yourselves: it is the gift of God: not of works, lest any man should boast (Ephesians 2:4-9).

AMEN. "So let it be!"

I hope this has been a helpful insight into God's Word. All of us in Christ are victors!

Amen and Amen!

REVELATION STUDY

CHRIST

Introduction
Revelation 1:1-3

Vision of Christ
Revelation 1:4-20

7 CHURCHES

Ephesus > Smyrna > Pergamos > Thyatira > Sardis > Philadelphia > Laodicea

RAPTURE

7 SEALS

Peace
War
Famine
Death
Martyrs
Destruction
Silence

7 TRUMPETS

Hail, Fire, Blood
Falling Meteor
Falling Star
Sun, Moon, Stars
Demon Locusts
Satan's Army
Two Witnesses
Earthquake

7 PERSONALITIES

Man Child 12:5-6
Michael 12:7-12
Antichrist 13:1-10
False Prophet 13:11-18
Red Dragon 12:3-4
Woman Clothed in Sun 12:1-2
144,000 Jews 14:1-5

7 MESSENGERS

GOSPEL
BABYLON IS FALLEN
MARK OF THE BEAST
BLESSED ARE THE DEAD
REAP
PREPARE THE HARVEST
HARVEST TIME

7 VIALS

Boils 16:1-2
Sea to Blood 16:3
Rivers to Blood 16:4-7
Oppressive Heat 16:8-9
Darkness 16:10-11
Euphrates Dries Up 16:12-16
Hail 16:17-21

7 DOOMS

Religious Babylon
Commercial Babylon
Marriage Supper of the Lamb
Beast
False Prophet
Nations
Millennium
Satan
Wicked of all Ages

Made in United States
Orlando, FL
15 May 2022

17891728R00202